Start a Business Today

5 Unique Business Ideas You Can Start Right Now

ADAM ROSE

ADAM ROSE

Published by A&T Publishing

First Edition: 2024

Paperback ISBN: 978-1-7385332-6-8
eBook ISBN: 978-1-7385332-5-1

Books from Author

9 Money Habits Keeping you Poor

My Story to Financial Freedom

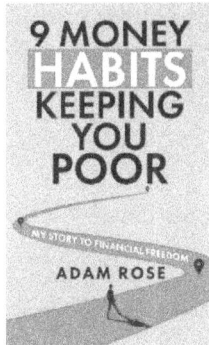

Unique Daily Quotes

Over 100 Inspirational and Motivational Quotes
for Entrepreneurs

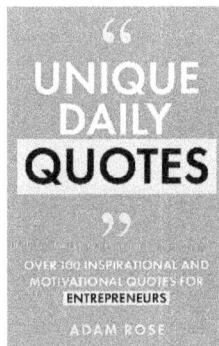

To the visionaries and the fearless,

For daring to dream and taking the leap,

May these pages ignite your passion,

And empower you to turn ideas into reality.

Contents

Introduction

Imagine a life full of endless possibilities where you are the architect of your destiny and financial freedom isn't a dream but a tangible part of your everyday existence. Picture waking up each day and working exactly how you want. Envision having the power to shape your future and those of your loved ones, while also creating a positive impact on the world. This book is your guide to turning this vision into reality.

This is the kind life I also wanted. Through perseverance and hard work, I discovered how to build sustainable wealth, which inspired me to help other aspiring entrepreneurs on their journeys to build their own businesses the right way. The world needs entrepreneurs, and building a business the right way means doing it on your terms and providing value in ways that bring you joy. By the end of this book, you will learn to achieve this in a way that brings you financial freedom for years to come.

I'm Adam, and I'm here to empower you to break free from the shackles of traditional employment and embrace the endless opportunities that come with entrepreneurship.

I've experienced all the ups and downs firsthand. From failing in business to achieving success and living the life of an entrepreneur, I'm here to help you flatten your learning curve when it comes to starting a business and testing out the viability of different ideas. To put it simply, I've walked the path of what I preach. From humble beginnings to running multiple businesses throughout my life, I know all about both successes and failures and how to make the most of both. But beyond mere credentials, my passion lies in empowering entrepreneurs like you to seize control of their destinies with confidence.

In my last book, *9 Money Habits Keeping You Poor*, we discussed the nine financial habits that keep people in poverty and how to break past them for true fulfillment. Now that we've developed the foundation of a financial mindset, we will go even deeper into an entrepreneurial mindset and the actionable ways to build a thriving business for the long term.

Throughout this comprehensive guide, you will:

- Discover the tools necessary to become a successful entrepreneur

- Follow a step-by-step guide on how to launch a business

- Acquire effective strategies to kickstart your entrepreneurial journey

- Unlock the secrets to crafting a business venture that not only thrives but endures

- Gain inspiration from 5 unique and exciting business ideas you can start today

When it comes to success, it's not only about having great ideas but also executing them. This is why I'll provide you with practical advice and clear steps to ensure you can build a business with confidence and clarity. From evaluating your most-loved business ideas to setting achievable goals and persisting in the face of common setbacks, you'll be equipped with the skills and strategies needed to thrive in any entrepreneurial endeavor you choose.

In addition, this book is split into three distinct parts. In part one, we will get *ready for business*, honing in on developing an entrepreneurial mindset and examining how we can view the process of building a business to achieve the greatest sense of fulfillment. Additionally, we will explore the importance of starting a business amidst the current volatile economic climate and define a business system, emphasizing why it is essential to your entrepreneurial plan.

In part 2, we will move on to *starting your business* and develop a detailed framework on how to construct a business idea. We will then discuss specific business ideas and how to test the viability of each and build your business from scratch. With each idea, we will examine innovative ways to build that business, each accompanied by practical insights and success stories to guide your path.

In part 3, we will map out your *future business* and set you up for success. We will discuss the importance of staying focused on your goals, drawing from the wisdom of those who've built similar empires before. We will understand the correct way to fail and focus on the meaning of being a value-centric entrepreneur.

To get the most out of this book and the actionable strategies mentioned, take notes, and write down any insights that inspire you along the way. This will be especially important in part 2, where we assess the specific ways to build your ideal business from scratch. You'll be able to answer reflective questions throughout this book that will help you define your path, and you'll also be able to jot down techniques and resources to aid you in the process of building your business.

The time for action is now. Will you watch from the sidelines as other entrepreneurs take control of their lives? Or will you join us in the exhilarating adventure of building a business? The choice is yours, but remember, true transformation begins with a single step. I invite you to commit wholeheartedly to this journey, embrace the challenges and opportunities ahead, and together, let's create a promising and prosperous future for all.

Part One: Getting Ready for Business

66

"You **can**, you **should**, and if you're brave enough to start, you **will**."

– STEPHEN KING –

Chapter 1: Start a Business or Die

Deep down, I've always felt that playing it safe isn't the best choice, yet I haven't been able to push myself to take bigger risks. Sitting at my desk in my cramped cubicle, staring at the flickering fluorescent lights above, I couldn't shake the feeling of discontent that haunted me day in and day out. The monotony of my 9-to-5 job at the car dealership felt suffocating, like a heavy weight pressing down on my chest, reminding me of the dreams I had yet to chase.

With my wonderful wife Thea and three amazing children depending on me, the responsibility of providing for my family weighed heavily on me. But as I scrolled through success stories of entrepreneurs who had turned their visions into reality, I couldn't ignore my intuition urging me to take the same leap.

I knew that my long-term life goals couldn't be met with my current job. It felt like a suffocating kind of comfort. The security of my job seemed like a death sentence because I needed more. I wanted the satisfaction of increasing my income whenever I pleased instead of waiting years to be promoted to a new position with a capped salary.

It felt like a ticking time bomb. My expenses were steadily rising day by day, surpassing my income. It was only a matter of time before I would have more money going out than coming in. This daunting reality hit me like a ton of bricks! I knew I couldn't continue on this doomed trajectory.

I was at a crossroads. I could continue trading my time for a paycheck that barely covered the bills, or I could embrace the freedom, challenges, and the exhilarating potential of entrepreneurship. I could constantly budget and become poorer as my salary failed to keep up with inflation, or I could embrace the innovation of owning a business and the opportunities to increase my income whenever I pleased.

With each passing day, I became more convinced that I was meant for something greater. I devoured inspiring statistics and success stories, finding hope in the opportunities that awaited those bold enough to seize them. I learned that 65.3% of small businesses are profitable and that 9% of small businesses make over $1 million (United States Census Bureau)! Quite the contrary to what you typically hear about entrepreneurship.

As I reflected on my time at the dealership thus far, I couldn't help but feel trapped despite the somewhat decent income. While earning a low six-figure salary may have provided me and my family with a sense of stability, it also came with its own set of limitations and frustrations. Ironically, I lacked security, feeling as though I could be let go at any moment. I lived paycheck to paycheck and felt like a slave to my job and the larger economic conditions around me.

No matter how hard I worked or how many hours I put in, there was always a limit on how much I could earn and how far I could advance. Starting my own business could allow me to diversify my income streams and build a foundation of financial stability that isn't reliant on any single source. As we all know, one of the main habits that keep us poor is limiting our streams of income. I had to diversify or let my long-term dreams die. Yes, I had a steady paycheck, but my dependency on that one paycheck left me vulnerable. Ironically, I believed that the freedom of being a business owner would give me a new type of stability that came from multiple sources. By becoming an entrepreneur, I could escape the limitations of a fixed salary and explore the potential for wealth creation through owning and managing a successful business. With strategic planning and dedication, my potential earnings and financial abundance have no limits at all.

I couldn't shake the lack of autonomy and control over my destiny. I was often at the mercy of someone else's agenda, with little say in how my time and talents were utilized. Starting a business would allow me to chart my own course, make decisions that align with my values, and take control of my daily schedule. I wanted to spend more time doing what I loved—traveling, spending time with my family, and working on things that I was passionate about and that made a difference to the world. At this point, I knew my 9-to-5 was the problem. *Starting a business became a matter of life and death.* If I wanted to achieve financial freedom, I could never reach it by being an employee; I had to *create a business.*

But as I contemplated the decision to start my own business, no matter how many success stories I saw, I couldn't ignore the discouraging statistics about the success rates of small businesses. In reality, launching a business requires a significant amount of grit and resilience. It's not enough to simply have a good idea; you also need the drive and determination to see it through, even when the odds are stacked against you. Of course, you'll be great at what you do, but the skill of running a business is a different talent all on its own. Also, while not every small business will succeed, many do, and the rewards can be significant for those who can overcome the obstacles along the way.

Ultimately, you have to want to escape your current situation. If you don't feel like it's a matter of life and death, you may not be in the place to make the radical changes that starting a business requires. When it comes to entrepreneurship, nothing can be half-hearted. You must go all in.

I embarked on this journey with a mix of optimism and realism, which is what starting a business is all about. I knew that the road ahead would be tough, but I also believed in my ability to conquer any challenges that came my way.

It's Time to Change Your Life by Starting a Business

"If you push through that feeling of being scared, that feeling of taking a risk, really amazing things can happen."
– Marissa Mayer –

If you're still wondering if you have the drive needed to succeed, ask yourself the following questions:

- Are traditional careers killing your entrepreneurial spirit and leaving you feeling imprisoned?

- Are your long-term life goals only achievable with the flexibility and freedom offered by business systems compared to a 9-to-5 job?

- Are you willing to dedicate the time and effort to build a successful business, even if it means sacrificing other aspects of your life?

Let's review the problems that an employee faces and how they can be solved by starting a business.

Employment	Entrepreneurship
Confined to a narrow skill set and not doing what you love.	Unlimited avenues to pursue passions and align your actions with your values.
Capped salary and living paycheck to paycheck.	An abundance of diverse income opportunities and unlimited income potential.
Constantly budgeting and living frugally.	Expanding your means and gaining financial freedom.
Fear of losing your job.	Complete job security while in control of your destiny.
Victim of economic conditions and becoming poorer long term.	Opportunity to protect yourself from volatility and buffer yourself from external factors.
Lack of control over work schedule.	Work where and when you want.
Limited family and leisure time.	Freedom to choose how you spend your time.
Restricted social connections.	Expand and connect with a greater, unlimited network.

To change your circumstances, you must have a strong sense of this reality and feel intense agitation and frustration.

This burning desire will fuel your change and keep you motivated on your road to entrepreneurship.

While the benefits of being an entrepreneur are enticing, starting a business cannot be a casual side hobby—you must give it your *all* to succeed. Significant time sacrifices in the beginning are necessary, especially in the initial stages of setting up the back end of your business. You may know how to succeed in your business industry, but setting up a business from scratch is a new skill that you'll have to learn and dedicate your time to. As you know, businesses are competitive. You must work harder and smarter than everyone else to maintain a competitive edge. With all of that being said, the rewards of being a business owner will outweigh the pain you've been experiencing at your current job. If you're willing to make the shift and give it your all, you have a real shot at finding success.

If you truly believe that the life you dream of can only be done by owning a business, then congratulations, you're in the right place. Success in entrepreneurship is more than just having a great idea—it's about having the passion, perseverance, and determination to see it through. With the right mindset and a willingness to embrace the challenges that lie ahead, I have no doubt you will achieve great things with your new business. In the next chapter, we will go over your answers to the earlier questions and brainstorm ways to develop a successful business owner mindset before starting your journey.

Key Takeaways

- The biggest risk is not taking any risk. Entrepreneurship involves uncertainty, but it also offers opportunities for growth and success that can't be found in traditional employment.

- Trust your intuition guiding you toward entrepreneurship to achieve unlimited growth potential compared to traditional employment.

- Acknowledge the limitations of traditional employment in providing both financial security and autonomy over your destiny, which is unlimited when it comes to owning a business.

- Your current limits and financial challenges can only be overcome through entrepreneurship, not employment.

- Ponder the importance of pursuing passions and finding meaning in work, which entrepreneurship can provide.

- To start and thrive in business, you must make it a matter of life or death. You cannot be half-hearted and must recognize the necessity of full commitment to entrepreneurship.

66

"The entrepreneur always **searches** for **change**, **responds** to it, and **exploits** it as an **opportunity**."

– PETER DRUCKER –

Chapter 2: From Consumer to Creator

Think Like an Entrepreneur

Among the most inspiring entrepreneurs of our time is Sara Blakely, the visionary behind Spanx. Faced with the frustration of an unsolved problem, she chose not to go through the absence of a solution but to become the solution herself.

Her revolutionary shapewear brand came to her in a moment of inspiration. She was getting ready for a party and wanted to wear a pair of cream-colored pants. However, she struggled to find the right undergarment that would give her a seamless look.

In a moment of frustration, she decided to take matters into her own hands. She grabbed a pair of scissors and cut the feet off a pair of pantyhose, creating a makeshift undergarment that would smooth out her silhouette without the discomfort of traditional shapewear. She wore the improvised garment to the party and was amazed by the results.

This experience sparked a lightbulb moment for her. She realized there was a gap in the market for comfortable and effective shapewear that could provide women with a flattering silhouette without sacrificing comfort. She saw an opportunity to create a product that would empower women and boost their confidence.

Her story, from a wardrobe malfunction to a global empire, is the prime example of shifting our gaze from consumption to creation. It's time to embrace challenges as opportunities and start thinking like an entrepreneur. This kind of entrepreneurial mindset has the power to shape our own destinies and transform the world around us.

In a world filled with messages of consumption, where ready-made solutions often seem to take over innovation, entrepreneurs remain committed to challenging the status quo. They are the creators, the visionaries who not only perceive the problems but create the solutions.

When we think about building a business, we must switch from being a *consumer* to a *creator*. We must explore what makes up an entrepreneurial mindset—a mindset that distinguishes between merely using the product or service of someone's hard work and cultivating the seeds of our own enterprise. Visionary entrepreneurs have the ability to transform challenges into opportunities and, in turn, their visions into reality.

As Idowu Koyenikan once said, "Success comes from the inside out. In order to change what is on the outside, you must first change what is on the inside." This journey goes beyond acquiring external success and money and is about fostering resilience, creativity, and visions that propel us toward our entrepreneurial aspirations.

Building an Entrepreneurial Mindset

"Entrepreneurs have a mindset that sees the possibilities
rather than the problems created by change."

– J. Gregory Dees –

What makes an entrepreneur? The entrepreneurial mindset is not a set of personality traits or abilities reserved for a select few. It is a tangible framework of thought, a cognitive paradigm that distinguishes entrepreneurs from the rest of the population. It's a train of thought you can obtain and build yourself.

At its core, the entrepreneurial mindset encompasses a unique blend of creativity, resilience, adaptability, and a penchant for calculated risk-taking. Research into the science behind this mindset reveals fascinating insights into the inner workings of the entrepreneurial brain and the psychology behind entrepreneurial behavior.

For instance, studies have shown that entrepreneurs exhibit greater neural plasticity—the brain's ability to reorganize itself in response to new situations or experiences—compared to non-entrepreneurs. This heightened neuroplasticity allows entrepreneurs to readily adapt to changing environments and innovate in the face of adversity.

Neuroscientific research has also demonstrated that entrepreneurs have distinct patterns of brain activity when assessing risk and reward. Contrary to popular belief, entrepreneurs do not have a higher tolerance for risk per se; rather, they exhibit a unique neural response that weighs potential rewards more heavily than potential losses. Our neural responses are always adjustable, and you can also develop this type of neural response! This differential processing of risk and reward motivates entrepreneurs to take calculated risks and pursue opportunities with significant gains. Entrepreneurial thinking is also characterized by a propensity for creativity and divergent thinking—the ability to generate multiple solutions to a problem and think outside the box. Studies have found that entrepreneurs score higher on measures of creativity and exhibit greater cognitive flexibility compared to non-entrepreneurs, which goes hand in hand with neural plasticity. This enables entrepreneurs to envision novel solutions, disrupt industries, and pioneer groundbreaking innovations like Spanx.

As we know, entrepreneurship is inherently fraught with uncertainty, setbacks, and failures. Yet, entrepreneurs possess a remarkable capacity for determination and grit. Research has shown that resilient individuals are more likely to succeed in entrepreneurial endeavors, bouncing back from failures stronger and more determined than before (which we will discuss later in the book). This just goes to show how important mindset is when it comes to building a business.

However, it's not *all* internal. The environment in which entrepreneurs operate plays a pivotal role in shaping their mindset and behavior. Entrepreneurial success flourishes in ecosystems that combine access to capital, mentorship, networking opportunities, and supportive communities. These elements create an ideal environment for innovation and growth. Studies have demonstrated the significant impact of social networks and peer influence on entrepreneurial decision-making, highlighting the importance of surrounding oneself with like-minded individuals and mentors.

These statistics and findings underscore the multidimensional nature of the entrepreneurial mindset—a fusion of cognitive, emotional, and environmental factors that catalyze entrepreneurial success. All these factors are attainable. Through understanding the science behind the entrepreneurial mindset, aspiring entrepreneurs can develop these essential attributes, harness their innate potential, and confidently navigate the intricate path of entrepreneurship.

Consumer Vs. Producer Mindset

"Producers spend money on investment, Consumers spend money on distraction."
– John Macdonald –

One of the first steps toward cultivating these entrepreneurial qualities is to understand the difference between a *consumer* and *producer* mindset. While the consumer mindset gravitates toward consumption and seeking fulfillment through goods and experiences, the producer mindset embodies creation, innovation, and value generation. The mindset we choose to have (because, yes, it is a choice) not only delineates our actions but also influences our perception of the world.

To understand the distinction between these two mindsets, we'll analyze the table below. Take a moment to reflect on which mindset you tend to adopt more often and how you may be able to shift from being a consumer to a producer.

Consumer Mindset	Producer Mindset
Seeks ready-made solutions to fulfill immediate needs.	Identifies problems as opportunities for innovation.
Passively consumes products and services without question.	Actively creates value and contributes to society.
Sees the world from an individual lens and focuses on their own specific desires.	Has a broad view of the world and sees the collective nature and needs of people and society.
Fears failure and making mistakes.	Sees failure as a necessary learning opportunity and reaps the benefit from it.
Lacks ownership and responsibility for life's problems and challenges.	Proactively takes accountability and responsibility for any obstacles experienced in life.
Follows trends and seeks validation from others.	Sets trends and forges new paths with conviction.

Consumer Mindset	Producer Mindset
Conforms to societal norms and expectations.	Challenges the status quo and embraces change.

Are you content with passive consumption or aspire to become an active producer? Consider the following:

- Do I tend to seek out pre-packaged solutions rather than exploring innovative alternatives?

- Am I comfortable relying on others for guidance, or do I take the initiative to solve problems independently?

- Should I prioritize my personal needs and desires, or should I have a greater awareness of others and broader societal issues?

- Do I passively consume information and media without critically evaluating its validity and relevance?

- Have I succumbed to societal pressures and conformity, or am I brave enough to challenge conventional wisdom and pursue my own path, like starting a business?

The prevalence of consumerism in society can be attributed to many psychological and social causes. From early childhood, we are inundated with messages that equate consumption with happiness and success. Advertising, peer pressure, and societal norms reinforce the notion that acquiring material possessions and indulging in instant gratification are the keys to fulfillment. As we explored in *9 Money Habits Keeping You Poor*, this leads to habit #3: thoughtless spending. Not only does this prevent you from making your entrepreneurial ideas come to life, but it also prevents you from becoming wealthier in the long term.

Consumerism is appealing because of its simplicity and convenience. It requires minimal effort and offers immediate gratification, making it attractive to anyone seeking comfort and security. However, this reliance on consumption and fitting in comes at a cost, as it diminishes our capacity for initiative, innovation, and self-reliance.

On the contrary, having a producer mindset embodies the spirit of entrepreneurship. It involves the willingness to embrace challenges, take calculated risks, and create value for oneself and others. While everyone is a consumer to some extent, the distinguishing characteristic of successful entrepreneurs is that they produce *more* than they consume. Little by little, we can all make the shift from a consumer to a producer, going past passive consumption and more toward self-discovery, innovation, and creation.

At the heart of this transition lies a shift in perspective—from viewing problems as obstacles to viewing them as opportunities for creation and innovation. Real entrepreneurs turn challenges into springboards for success. Consider Mark Zuckerberg, the visionary behind Facebook, who identified the opportunity to connect people in an increasingly digital world and created a social networking platform that revolutionized communication and connectivity.

Problem-solving and opportunity-seeking go hand in hand. In addition to providing products or services, entrepreneurs are in the business of solving problems. Henry Ford didn't just manufacture cars; he solved the problem of inefficient transportation by revolutionizing the automotive industry by introducing of the assembly line and mass production techniques. Apple doesn't merely produce phones and gadgets; it solves the problem of communication, entertainment, and productivity by designing seamlessly integrated devices and software ecosystems that enhance the lives of millions.

It's the same way in your own life—you give someone money in return for a solution to a problem you're experiencing. For example, you pay a supermarket for the convenience of packaging and organizing food items in a convenient way, which solves the basic human need for sustenance. Similarly, you exchange money for clothes from a brand to make you look and feel good or subscribe to Netflix to alleviate your boredom.

At its core, entrepreneurship is about identifying unmet needs, addressing pain points, and delivering value to consumers (we will delve into this further in Chapter 12). Products and services are manifestations of this underlying goal— the means through which problems are solved and opportunities are seized. People will pay *you* to solve their problems, and that is the essence of entrepreneurship.

How to Capitalize on Entrepreneurial Opportunities

"Most innovation involves doing the things we do every day a little bit better rather than creating something completely new and different."

– Darin Bifani –

In the process of building a business and trying to find success as an entrepreneur, identifying and capitalizing on opportunities is a great way to get your brain working toward that entrepreneurial mindset. Keep in mind that this journey is not made of shortcuts or cheat codes; it requires diligence, foresight, and a willingness to embrace the process. This includes experimentation and many ideas that may never fully come to life. So, let's look at some ways that you can begin to uncover opportunities and navigate the entrepreneurial landscape with perseverance.

- **Do Market Research and Trend Analysis:** Understanding market dynamics and consumer trends is essential for identifying untapped opportunities. Conduct market research to identify emerging needs, gaps in the market, and areas ripe for disruption. If you're already interested in starting a business, you'll likely find this fascinating. Stay up-dated on industry trends, technological advance-ments, and shifting consumer preferences to stay ahead of the curve and identify new opportunities as they arise.

- **Embrace a Problem-Solving Approach:** Adopt a problem-solving mindset and seek out challenges that present opportunities for innovation. Look for pain points and inefficiencies in existing systems, processes, and industries. By creatively addressing these problems, you can carve out a niche and dif-ferentiate yourself from competitors when you build your business.

- **Network and Collaborate with Other Innova-tors:** Forge strategic partnerships and leverage your current network to uncover hidden opportunities. Surround yourself with mentors, advisors, and peers who can offer valuable insights, connections, and support. Collaborate with businesses and individuals whose strengths complement your own. By pooling resources and sharing expertise, you can amplify your impact and achieve more than you could on your own. When you surround yourself with other producers, you help strengthen and maintain your entrepreneurial mindset.

- **Continuously Learn & Adapt:** Stay curious, agile, and open-minded in your entrepreneurial journey. Continuously seek out new knowledge, skills, and experiences to adapt to changing circumstances and evolving market dynamics. Be willing to pivot and iterate based on feedback, data, and insights gleaned from your experiences. A major aspect of entrepreneurship is continuous experimentation.

- **Embody Perseverance and Resilience:** Embrace the inevitable setbacks, failures, and challenges along the entrepreneurial journey. Cultivate resilience by reframing obstacles as opportunities for growth and learning. Focus on long-term goals and stay committed to your vision, even in the face of challenges.

Embrace the endless chances to create value for the world and adopt an entrepreneurial mindset to build a business with clarity, confidence, and purpose. Remember, there are no shortcuts to success; it is the journey itself—the process of discovery, growth, and providing value—that defines the entrepreneurial experience.

Key Takeaways

- Transitioning from passive consumption to active creation is essential for entrepreneurial success. Let go of the consumer mindset and embrace the mindset of a producer who identifies problems as opportunities for a solution.

- Look for unmet needs and inefficiencies in the market and innovate solutions that deliver value to consumers.

- Stay agile and open-minded. Adapt to changing circumstances and market dynamics, iterating on your ideas based on feedback and insights.

- Remember that entrepreneurship is about solving problems, not just providing products or services. Focus on addressing consumer needs and pain points, ensuring you deliver meaningful solutions.

- Surround yourself with others who strengthen your entrepreneurial mindset and those who enable you to magnify your impact.

66

"True **business** owners can go on vacation forever because they own a **system**, not a job. If the business owner is on vacation, the **money** still comes in."

– ROBERT KIYOSAKI –

Chapter 3: The Engine of Wealth
Building a Business System

When I began my car detailing business, I thought I was finally breaking free from the constraints of traditional employment. I was my own boss and called the shots. But as the days went by, I found myself stuck in a familiar cycle, one that didn't seem far off from my days as a car salesperson. Despite being the owner of my business, I was still the one doing everything—managing operations, performing admin tasks, and even handling some of the jobs myself. In fact, I was doing a lot more than when I was a salesperson!

Although I had successfully set up a thriving business, the shackles I was trying to break free from were still holding me down. It didn't take long for me to realize that I hadn't yet escaped the employee mindset. Instead, I transitioned into a different role with similar demands and even more tasks to handle now that I was in control of everything. I went from being *employed* to *self-employed*, which didn't allow me to realize my dreams of true financial freedom. If I wanted to liberate myself and scale my business to new heights, I needed to free up my time. The only way to do that was to build a *system*.

So, I set out to implement a comprehensive training program for my staff and brought in management to handle the day-to-day operations that didn't need my time. By delegating responsibilities and automating processes, I was able to grow my business while simultaneously freeing up my own time. Building this system marked the beginning of my journey toward reaping the true benefits of entrepreneurship. Having a business isn't enough; you must build a *business system* detached from your time to achieve the freedom you desire.

In this chapter, we'll go over one of the most important fundamentals of building a business: creating a sustainable business system that acts as an engine of wealth. We'll also discuss the differences between a business system and a money system and their individual roles in achieving financial independence.

A Business System Vs. A Money System

"When money realizes that it is in good hands, it wants to stay and multiply in those hands."

– Idowu Koyenikan –

Financial freedom is attained when your passive income surpasses your expenses, which was discussed in detail in *9*

Money Habits Keeping You Poor. Both the business system and the money system play crucial roles in achieving this goal.

A money system involves putting your money to work to create wealth. This is essentially investing in assets that generate income, such as real estate, stocks, and commodities. On the other hand, a business system involves creating a scalable business that can generate wealth independent of your time.

A money system demands a substantial initial monetary investment and offers relatively modest returns, typically 5–10%. However, it requires minimal time investment to get started and to maintain momentum. In contrast, a business system requires time and effort to establish and less initial monetary investment, but it holds the potential for unlimited wealth generation, as discussed in Chapter 1.

Your business system, therefore, serves as your primary wealth engine, generating the funds needed to power your money system. This, in turn, becomes the source of your passive income, paving the way to financial autonomy!

Business System

Active Income

Money System

Assets
- Real estate
- Stocks
- Commodities

Passive Income

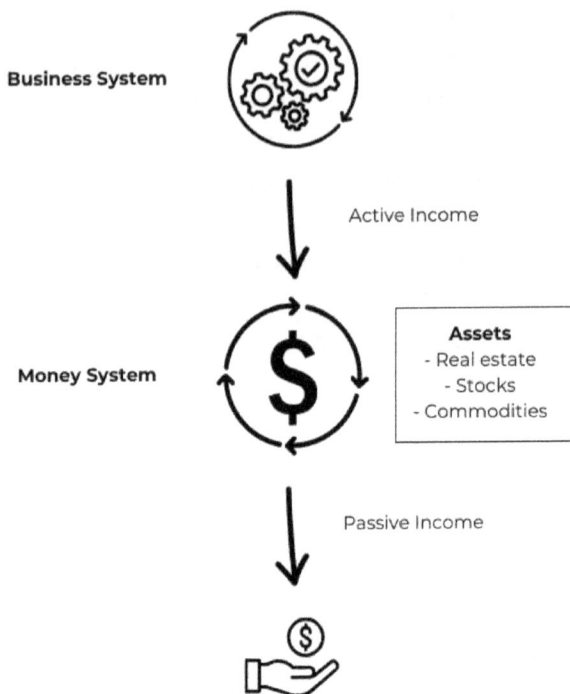

Fig 1: Illustrates the relationship between your business system and money system.

While creating a business system may seem daunting and grand, you can still start a business system alongside your current job and turn it into your full-time gig as you gain momentum. Becoming an entrepreneur is a journey, and there are different paths to achieving your objectives. It is often quite sensible and responsible to continue in your current employment and start your business as a side hustle and go full-time once it's sufficiently established. The important thing is that if you apply the principles we will discuss, you will be on the right path to financial success.

The Only Roadmap to Financial Freedom

"If you want to be financially free, you need to become a different person than you are today and let go of whatever has held you back in the past."

– Robert Kiyosaki –

Investing in assets is undeniably a crucial aspect of building wealth, and relying solely on a money system is insufficient for achieving a life of financial freedom. Likewise, relying on a business system is a critical aspect of generating wealth; however, it doesn't allow you to achieve long-term financial stability on its own. You must implement *both* systems as part of your plan to achieve financial freedom.

Investing alone won't yield enough passive income to sustain a life of financial freedom—at least not within a reasonable timeframe. Sure, the power of compounding can work wonders over decades, which is why people often think about compounding in terms of their retirement savings, but who wants to wait 50 years before reaping the rewards? Small money doesn't make big money, *big money makes big money.*

For instance, investing in the stock market has historically yielded significant returns over time for many people, but it requires a substantial initial investment. According to Investopedia, it takes an average of 16 to 20 years for an investment in the stock market to double in value (Kenton, 2015). You also need a sizable amount of capital to achieve this type of meaningful growth in your investments. Therefore, if you invest in different stocks and mutual funds in the hope of becoming financially independent, you may generate some passive income through those investments but will soon realize that it isn't enough to cover your daily expenses and give you the lifestyle you truly want. The purpose of investing is to protect and grow your wealth, not generate wealth.

You cannot just rely on your business system to sustain your desired lifestyle. Although it generates substantial active income, it will always require some of your time to manage and maintain. More importantly, the business system can become obsolete over time due to a changing world and customer needs. Therefore, your active income from your business system must be invested to generate passive income from your money system. Passive income is the ultimate measure of financial freedom because you don't want your income tied to your time.

Let's consider a simple example to determine the amount of capital required to meet your passive income target solely through investing. If we set a pre-tax monthly income of $10,000 and work with an 8% annual return, we would need a base capital amount of $1.5 million. Assuming we start with $100,000, it would take us 36 years before we reach a capital base of $1 million. Even if you were to supplement your investments with an extra $20,000 per year from your salary, it would still take you 21 years to reach that goal.

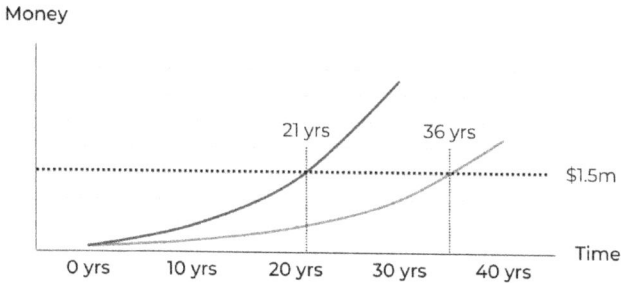

Fig 2: The chart shows the capital growth to reach our target capital base of $1.5 million for both investment strategy examples.

This is where building a business system comes into play. Unlike investments, a business system offers the opportunity for dynamic growth. This potential allows you to generate the wealth required to fuel your money system to produce the results needed to meet your passive income targets.

Look at another example in which our business consistently generates a surplus of $10,000 a month. We allocate this surplus toward our regular investment fund to fuel our money system. Starting with the same $100,000 it would take eight years to hit our passive income target of $10,000 a month.

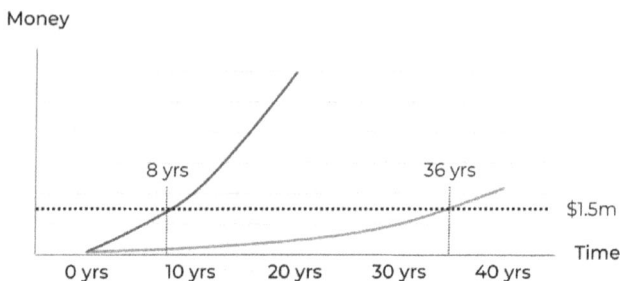

Fig 3: The chart shows the capital growth to reach our target capital base of $1.5 million based on the additional $10,000 per month surplus from our business.

When I started my journey as an investor and entrepreneur, I had some success in real estate and built an impressive portfolio over time. However, financial freedom was still out of reach for my family and me, as the returns from my investments did not meet the passive income target I needed to truly be free. I knew I had to increase the investment amount through businesses to achieve my goals. It was only once I started my car detailing business and scaled it through a system that I realized my dreams.

The key takeaway here is that while a money system is an essential component of your financial roadmap, it's not sufficient for achieving long-term financial freedom. Building a business system is crucial for creating sustainable wealth, offering scalability, adaptability, and the potential for exponential growth.

You Cannot Be THE Business

"Let systems run the business and people run the systems.
People come and go but the systems remain constant."
– Michael Gerber –

It's important to note that an individual cannot function as the entirety of a business. While it's true that many entrepreneurs start out by wearing multiple hats and taking on various roles within their ventures, there comes a point where they need extra help. This is very common with business owners who initially work as freelancers.

For instance, if you're a freelance graphic designer, you'll likely begin by handling every aspect of your business single-handedly. From client acquisition to project management to invoicing, you may eventually stretch yourself thin, struggling to keep up with the workload and sacrificing valuable time and energy in the process. You become the key person dependent for the business to operate. If you take a vacation or need a break, the business comes to a halt. Likewise, another person can't be a key dependency either. If you have a subject matter expert who is core to your business, you have the same problem. The success of your business and its longevity hinges on them.

At some point, all business owners and freelancers realize that there is a ceiling to their earning potential. You can only take on a finite number of projects at any given time, and your income is often directly tied to the number of hours you can put in. In most cases, you're trading your time for money—an unsustainable model that is inherently limiting in the long run. Therefore, the business you create must factor in the above limitations and not be restricted by them. We will discuss the criteria for selecting a business in detail in the next chapter.

But how do you know if you're a self-employed free-lancer, an entrepreneur, or something else? What are the differences between these various levels of owning a business?

Let's look at the differences between being employed, self-employed, and being an entrepreneur. These all involve different responsibilities and opportunities for wealth creation.

	Employed	Self-employed	Entrepreneur
Definition	Work for a company or organization under a contract of employment.	Work for oneself and manage all aspects of the business.	Create and operate your own business(es) to generate profit by creating value.
Responsibility	Defined roles and responsibilities within the organization.	Sole responsibility for finding clients, managing finances, and ensuring the success of the venture.	Identify opportunities, develop innovative solutions, and navigate the marketplace.
Wealth Creation	Limited opportunities for wealth creation compared to self-employed individuals and entrepreneurs.	Opportunities for wealth creation but limited by your time and effort.	Unlimited opportunities on creating long-term wealth and impact by scaling.

Differentiating between a business and a business system is important.

Business	Business System
Coffee shop: Individual owns and operates a small independent coffee shop.	Coffee Chain: Expanding beyond a single location to multiple outlets in different areas.
Web designer: Developer who works independently, building websites and web applications for clients.	Web design agency: Scaling up operations by hiring additional developers, designers, and project managers to handle larger projects and provide a broader range of web development services to clients.
Personal trainer: Works directly with clients in 1-2-1 or group sessions.	Personal training platform: Offers workout videos, nutrition plans, and merchandise online.

One of the biggest benefits of a business system is that you are creating an asset. If your business system becomes an asset, it has increased value and becomes attractive to investors. This could mean selling equity via shares in the business or the entire business for large sums of money. A business that isn't a system doesn't allow this, as the investment value is limited and tied to you or an individual. This should always be on every entrepreneur's long-term plan, having an exit. The "exit" allows you to realize the true value of the business system you have created, which is the ultimate goal. You can keep growing your income and get more of your time back by recognizing early on the importance of building a scalable business system. This will help you make the switch from being employed or self-employed to being a true entrepreneur. Rather than relying solely on your individual efforts, you can create processes, systems, and structures that could operate independently of your direct involvement.

By delegating tasks, hiring employees, and implementing automation tools, just like I did in my car detailing business, you can focus more on high-level strategic initiatives that drive growth and expansion. While self-employment may offer autonomy and flexibility, it often comes at the expense of scalability and long-term growth potential. On the other hand, building a business system allows for exponential growth and the creation of wealth beyond the confines of individual effort.

As I reflect on my journey as a car detailing entrepreneur to a business owner who now wears many hats, one thing becomes clear: building a sustainable business system is the foundation of long-term success. When I first ventured into entrepreneurship, I believed that being my own boss would liberate me from the constraints of traditional employment. However, I soon realized that true freedom requires more than just a business; it requires a system that can thrive and prosper regardless of individual contributions.

Key Takeaways

- While a money system offers modest returns with minimal time investment, a business system requires time and effort to establish but holds the potential for unlimited wealth generation.

- Building a business system is essential for creating sustainable wealth, offering scalability, adaptability, and the potential for exponential growth.

- A business system and money system work hand in hand as the roadmap to financial freedom.

- An individual cannot function as the entirety of a business, which is why transitioning from being self-employed to owning a scalable business system is vital.

Part Two: Starting Your Business

66

"**Money** never starts an idea; it is the **idea** that starts the money."

– WILLIAM J. CAMERON –

Chapter 4: How to Evaluate a Business Idea

Sitting at my desk, surrounded by swirling thoughts and scattered notes, I found myself at a crossroads that you've likely encountered as well. With a myriad of business ideas clamoring for attention and a market full of untapped opportunities, I knew there were tons of possibilities for the type of business I could build. However, they were all tied to the uncertainty of viability. Each idea was innovative, and I knew I could potentially fill each gap in the market, but I still felt paralyzed by indecision.

It was in this uncertainty that I began to dive deeper into understanding what constitutes a sustainable business. I needed a process to distinguish viable options and find a winning formula. By calibrating what I believed to be the fundamentals of entrepreneurship and aligning them with my vision of the life I wanted, I developed a set of criteria to navigate through potential business ideas. I achieved success by making sure that the business I built met these criteria.

When it comes to entrepreneurship, ideas are as common as stars in the night sky. But not every single flicker promises an entire constellation. Knowing the difference between flashes of inspiration and real opportunity is a skill honed through experience, observation, and an understanding of market dynamics. In this chapter, we'll dive into how to evaluate your business idea (or ideas) to know whether it's worth executing.

The success of a venture lies not merely in the initial idea but in how it provides value to society and whether it can continue to provide that in-demand value for years to come. However, indecision, often fueled by choice paralysis, often leaves aspiring entrepreneurs stranded in a sea of possibilities and ideas that they never actually execute. As stated in an article from *Forbes* regarding how decision fatigue can make or break a startup, "the larger the decision, the faster a person's energy depletes" (Gannon, 2022). This is why we must have a filtering system. A list of clear criteria removes the paralysis and simplifies the choices available to us. While it can be fun to daydream and brainstorm potential businesses, it's even more satisfying to create something, *knowing* that it will survive and thrive for years to come. The way to know this is by making sure it passes through all the necessary filters, which we'll be diving into in this chapter. This filtering system will tell you if your idea is worth executing or not.

However, as Scott Belsky, Adobe's chief product officer, said, "While ideas may serve as the seeds of innovation, it's execution that nurtures their growth." The distinction between success and stagnation often hinges not on the novelty of an idea but on how well it's executed. Although many entrepreneurs believe they have to invent the next iPhone, many successful businesses simply improve upon what's already there, which is known as *value tilt*. This is where you focus on a particular aspect of an existing product and service and improve it or offer something different, therefore tilting the value. One story that always inspires me is the way Van Leeuwen Ice Cream was executed and became a company. They transformed the flavor of a timeless pleasure, ice cream, by doing nothing more than changing a few of the main ingredients. When they only made a few thousand in their first year, they invested all of it back into their business. They expanded rapidly and now make over $300,000 a day. This is a prime example of executing an existing idea successfully.

Businesses also vary in terms of their size and structure. There is a spectrum of business systems ranging from small individual ventures, often referred to as *lifestyle* businesses, to large-scale enterprises known as *performance* businesses. A performance business is like Amazon or Uber, whereas a lifestyle business is like an online personal training platform or a writing agency started and managed by a single individual. The principles of a business system are applicable across this spectrum and are not limited to big corporations. A lifestyle business allows us to meet goals, such as freedom, security, and opportunities, as we discussed in Chapter 1, the same way a performance business does. Our focus will center on the development of lifestyle businesses, as that is what you will be creating.

Before diving into the specific business ideas in this book, let's differentiate between business models and a business idea. A business model outlines the framework within which a business operates, encompassing its revenue streams, value proposition, and key activities. On the other hand, a business idea represents a specific product, service, or concept that fulfills a market need using that business model. While we'll explore various business ideas, it's important to understand that the underlying business model can be applied to many different ideas. Once you understand the business ideas in this book and the models they are based on, you can easily apply them to other options of your choice.

Characteristics of a Business System

What exactly defines a business system? Let's outline the specific characteristics of a business system, and in the upcoming chapters, we'll review unique business ideas that meet these criteria. For now, keep in mind that any business idea you choose must fit these criteria to ensure that you are building a business system and not just a business, as we discussed in the last chapter.

To understand what makes a successful business, let's analyze **VANS**, a framework that outlines the four unique characteristics of a business system.

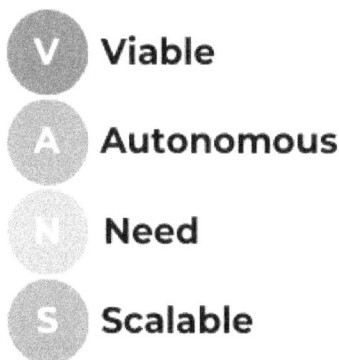

V **Viable**

A **Autonomous**

N **Need**

S **Scalable**

Viable: A business must be *viable*, meaning it is realistic for you to pursue, given your abilities, resources, and time constraints. Consider whether you have the necessary skills, access to resources, and time to bring the business idea to fruition. For example, if you're considering starting a graphic design business, assess whether you possess the design skills, access to design software and design professionals, and availability to take on client projects while managing things on the back end as you're just getting started. In addition, you need to ensure that the barrier to entry isn't too low to avoid too much competition and market saturation. The sweet spot is when you feel you are stretched and challenged to start the business but it remains within your capability to succeed.

Autonomous: Consider the time investment required to operate the business. A sustainable business should offer *autonomy*, allowing you to leverage your time effectively. Evaluate whether the business can be automated or delegated to minimize your direct involvement in day-to-day operations. The business must be able to produce income in the absence of your time. For example, an online course platform that delivers pre-recorded lectures and automated assessments allows instructors to reach a wide audience without being bound by time constraints, which is just one of the many great ways to create passive income. Of course, no income is fully passive, and this would still require time each week, but most of it could be automated, which is a sign that it's sustainable.

Need: A business must address a genuine *need* or fulfill a *market demand*. It should solve a problem or satisfy a desire within the target market. There may not be a glaring problem that has to be solved right away, and that's okay. As we can see with Van Leeuwen Ice Cream, nobody complained about the ingredients in ice cream, but the demand for an amazing dessert will always be high. What you don't want to do is create a business solely based on a personal hobby if there is no market interest for it. You may enjoy knitting, but it might prove difficult to scale into a business system. As Chris Rock said, "You can be anything you're good at — as long as they're hiring."

Conducting thorough market research is necessary to identify the needs and pain points of your potential customers, which we'll go over in later chapters. For instance, a meal delivery service targets busy professionals who need convenient and healthy meal options due to their hectic schedules.

Scalable: Finally, a business should be *scalable*, meaning it has the potential for growth and expansion without compromising its core structure or efficiency. Assess whether the business can accommodate increased demand, enter new markets, or introduce additional products or services over time. For instance, a software company that develops a scalable subscription-based product such as Microsoft Office 365, can easily onboard new users and expand its offerings with minimal incremental costs. Scaling this type of business is easier compared to a restaurant because it doesn't involve the high overhead costs of opening an entirely new location.

These four characteristics define a business system and therefore must be present in the business idea we choose to implement to reap the benefits that entrepreneurship offers.

The Growth Potential of Online Vs. Physical Businesses

"Ecommerce isn't the cherry on the cake, it's the new cake"

– Jean Paul Ago –

You may have already noticed that online businesses often fit the VANS criteria best. They are naturally aligned with the characteristics of being Autonomous and Scalable, as they sit on a technology-based platform and can reach global audiences seamlessly.

Even if you have an in-person business, the importance of an online presence can't be ignored! An online presence complements the traditional brick-and-mortar model by expanding reach, enhancing customer engagement, and providing additional revenue streams. By leveraging e-commerce platforms, social media channels, and digital marketing strategies, physical businesses can attract new customers, drive foot traffic to their stores, and differentiate themselves. Moreover, an online presence enables physical businesses to offer omnichannel experiences, allowing customers to transition between online and offline interactions.

Let's examine the different ways in which online versus physical businesses meet the VANS criteria.

Criteria	Online Business	Physical Business
Viable	Lower startup costs	Initial investment in physical space and higher maintenance costs
Autonomous	Potential for automation and scalability	Hands-on management and supervision but can utilize tech for efficiency
Need	Access to the vast online marketplace and niche markets	Capitalizes on local foot traffic but can still market to wider audiences online
Scalable	Expansion isn't physical, rapid scaling can meet growing demand	Strategic growth through franchising or multiple locations, limitations on geography

Scoring Metrics for Evaluation – Assessing Your Business Idea

Now, let's measure the feasibility, viability, and potential success of your idea. In the upcoming chapters, we'll use these scoring metrics to review and analyze various business ideas to help you make the best choice about which opportunity to pursue.

For each of the categories, we will be providing a score between 1 and 5, with 1 being the lowest score and 5 being the highest.

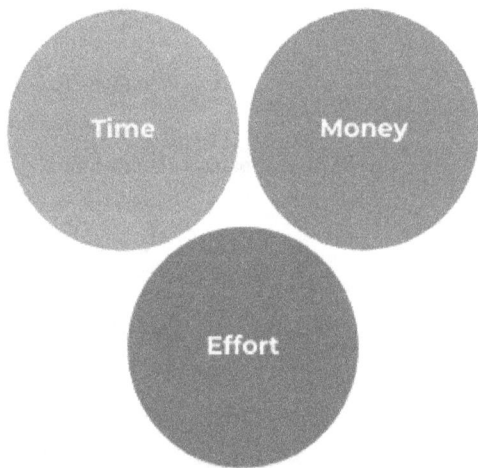

Let's dive into the three key categories for assessment:

Time to get started: Entrepreneurs spend an average of 69 hours (about three days) per week working on their businesses during the startup phase (Global Entrepreneurship Monitor, 2022). Time is a valuable resource, particularly during the initial stages of launching a business. Always evaluate the amount of time required to kickstart each business idea, including tasks such as research, planning, setup, and initial operations. Understanding the time commitment upfront enables you to allocate your resources efficiently and prioritize ideas that fit your schedule. If you already have a job, the time required to get started will be a crucial factor in selecting the right one for you.

Money to get started: Financial resources play a crucial role in turning a business idea into reality. Assess the upfront costs associated with each business idea, including equipment, inventory, marketing, and initial overhead. You can evaluate your readiness and identify potential funding sources or investment opportunities by evaluating requirements upfront. Additionally, early on in your entrepreneurial journey, you may want to experiment, learn, and try different models. You will want to do this quickly and cost-effectively as possible, so startup costs will be another critical factor in your decision-making process.

Effort to maintain: Beyond the initial setup phase, maintaining a business requires ongoing effort and commitment. Ensure you are evaluating the level of effort required to sustain each business idea over time, including tasks such as day-to-day operations, customer service, marketing, and growth strategies. By assessing the ongoing effort needed, you can gauge the scalability and long-term viability of your idea. This will also allow you to plan for staffing, automation, and outsourcing to streamline your operations.

Ultimately, evaluating your business ideas is both an art and a science. By applying the VANS criteria and scoring metrics, you can start to understand which of your ideas may be worth pursuing. For now, keep in mind that execution will always overpower ideation.

Key Takeaways

- Ideas are plentiful, but execution is paramount.

- A business system applies to any business size, be it a lifestyle or performance business.

- Understanding the distinction between a fleeting business idea and a sustainable business that can survive for years to come is essential.

- The VANS framework outlines key characteristics of a business system: Viable, Autonomous, Need, and Scalable.

- Online businesses often align well with the VANS criteria due to lower startup costs, scalability, and the ability to reach a global audience.

- Scoring metrics such as time, money, and effort are essential for evaluating business ideas and knowing which businesses will thrive in the long run.

66

"Digital content isn't **king**. It's the **kingdom**."

– LEE ODEN –

Chapter 5: Business Idea #1

Digital Products

Someone who has inspired me is Dave Chesson, a former naval officer turned bestselling author and savvy entrepreneur. While serving in the US Navy, he was deployed on an unaccompanied assignment to South Korea as a naval liaison officer, where he worked for two years away from his wife and kids. Little did he know that he was about to embark on a seven-figure side business.

Dave set out on a path to create a side income that would earn enough money for him to leave the military and be home with his family. He no longer wanted to miss birthdays or his kids' milestones. This led him to start writing books and self-publishing them online—an easy way to build a side business from the other side of the world. Using online book marketplaces, he earned over $275,000 from his books alone.

His success inspired him to create a marketing website for fellow publishers and research tools, to aid them in their self-publishing businesses. His marketing website garners

over 200,000 unique readers every month alone. From identifying niche markets to harnessing the potential of digital
marketing channels, Dave's digital product creation serves as
a blueprint for us in this chapter, where we'll learn how to
carve our own paths in the online commerce realm.

What are Digital Products?

When it comes to modern entrepreneurship, digital products
have emerged as new symbols of profitability. But what exactly constitutes a digital product? From eBooks to online
courses and software to subscription services, the realm of
digital products encompasses a wide range of offerings that
provide value to consumers. Some of the most popular include:

- **eBooks:** An eBook is a digital version of a book that
  can be read on electronic devices such as computers,
  tablets, or smartphones. Selling eBooks online is a
  great way to showcase your expertise on a particular
  topic or build a brand as a writer or business owner.
  They're also easy to create and distribute from any
  location with an internet connection.

- **Online courses:** An online course is a structured
  educational program delivered over the internet. It
  typically involves multimedia materials, lectures, as-
  signments, and assessments, which students can access remotely. Educational courses are another great

way to highlight your expertise on a particular topic and build a brand while earning passive income.

- **Design templates:** A design template is a premade layout or framework that provides a structure for creating consistent visual presentations or documents. It is often used in graphic design, web design, or document creation. Premade layouts for visual content creation are great for business owners who are selling design or other creative services.

- **Digital artwork:** Digital artwork refers to the creation of visual art using digital tools and techniques, such as digital drawing tablets, software programs, and computer graphics. This enables artists to produce and manipulate images entirely within a digital environment. Digital artwork businesses are great for artists or designers who want to sell their work after it's completed. Unlike design templates, digital artwork is typically more art focused.

- **Audio content:** Audio content is any consumable media conveyed through sound. This can include content like music samples, sounds effects, and voice overs. Producing and distributing audio content is also great for authors who release audiobooks or entrepreneurs who have podcasts.

In this chapter, you'll explore your first business idea, digital products, including what makes a digital product successful and how to evaluate its viability in the marketplace. By the end, you'll know how to create your own digital product business that stands the test of time.

At its core, a digital product is any intangible asset or service that is delivered electronically, often through digital channels such as the internet. The beauty of digital products lies in their versatility and scalability, offering entrepreneurs the opportunity to create innovative solutions with global reach.

Furthermore, digital product businesses offer several advantages over traditional physical businesses. They can be easily updated or modified based on customer feedback or changing market trends, providing continuous value to users. Additionally, digital distribution eliminates the need for inventory management, shipping, and storage, streamlining business operations and reducing overhead costs.

Consumers also increasingly prefer the convenience and accessibility of digital products. Whether it's learning a new skill through an online course, downloading digital artwork to decorate their walls, or streaming audio content on their favorite podcast platform, digital product businesses are now a way of life!

The demand for digital products is rapidly increasing and will only continue to grow in the years to come, according to experts. Market projections suggest significant growth and opportunity, with the e-learning sector poised to reach approximately $370 billion within the next few years (PR

Newswire, 2022). Digital products also offer high profit margins due to low production and distribution costs, resulting in large bottom-line returns. In fact, reports from Investopedia highlight profit margins exceeding 80% for many digital product businesses.

Scoring the Digital Product Business

It's no secret that the demand for digital products will only increase in the years to come, but how can you tell if a digital product business is worth pursuing compared to other ideas? Let's look at the time and financial investment required, as well as the ongoing effort needed to maintain the business on a scale of 1-5.

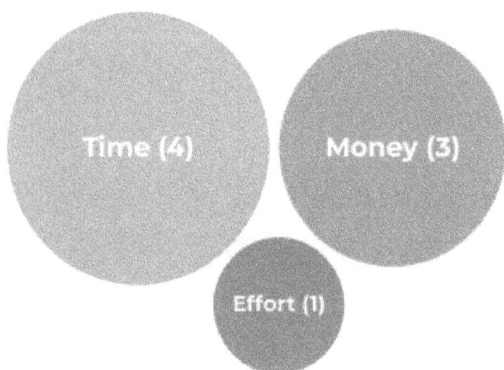

Time: 4/5

Creating a digital product demands upfront time commitment. Whether you're crafting an eBook, developing software, or curating multimedia content, each step requires planning, research, and execution. Time is also needed for testing, feedback incorporation, and troubleshooting any technical issues. However, once your digital product is launched, its shelf life can be extensive, potentially generating passive income for years to come with minimal ongoing time investment.

Money: 3/5

The financial investment required for a digital product business varies depending on the complexity and quality of the product. While it's possible to start with relatively little capital, investing more upfront can significantly enhance the product's quality and market appeal. Expenses may include software tools, outsourcing services (such as graphic design or content creation), marketing campaigns, and platform fees for hosting or distribution. However, the overhead costs are considerably lower compared to traditional brick-and-mortar businesses. Additionally, recurring expenses such as hosting fees or marketing campaigns may be necessary to sustain growth and visibility.

Effort:1/5

Once your digital product is created and made available to customers, the ongoing effort required for maintenance and support is minimal. Unlike physical products that demand inventory management, shipping logistics, and customer service, digital products can largely operate on autopilot. With automated delivery systems and digital distribution platforms handling transactions and customer access, you can focus on scaling, refining existing products, or even developing new ones. However, occasional updates, customer support inquiries, and marketing efforts to drive continued sales may necessitate some ongoing involvement.

Start a Digital Product Business

- Step 1: Market Research
- Step 2: Validating the Idea
- Step 3: Creating the Product
- Step 4: Launch and Iterate
- Step 5: Marketing and Promotion

Step 1: Market Research

Market research is essential for understanding your target audience's needs, preferences, and behaviors, as well as assessing your competitors and ways to stand out. Techniques for market research include:

- Identify target audience needs and preferences through surveys, interviews, or online forums. What problems does your target audience express about current digital products and how can you fill that gap with yours? You can figure this out by looking at Yelp reviews, Google reviews, and even online forums like Quora and Reddit to see how people discuss the other digital products available. Additional tools will be discussed below as well.

- Assess market competition to identify gaps and opportunities for differentiation. How will you maintain that competitive edge? Pay extra attention to 4-star reviews, as this means that someone almost loved the digital product, but they got one thing wrong. Perhaps your product can solve this problem and be the best out there.

- Conduct surveys or interviews with potential customers to gather feedback on product concepts and features. How can you make your product the best? You can do this by sending out automatic surveys to customers after they purchase your product or by requesting your email subscribers to complete a survey as well.

There are many free tools online that can help you conduct market research, including:

- **Google Keyword Planner:** This allows you to discover the search volume and competition level for specific keywords related to your niche. By analyzing relevant keywords related to existing digital products or the problems they aim to solve, you can understand what your target audience is searching for and then integrate those keywords throughout your marketing materials. That way, your business will show up on Google when they search for you!

- **SEMrush:** Provides comprehensive keyword research and competitive analysis features. You can use it to identify popular search queries related to your digital product niche and analyze the keywords your competitors are targeting.

- **AnswerThePublic:** This tool generates insights into the questions and topics people are searching for online. By entering relevant keywords related to your digital product niche, you can discover common queries and concerns that your target audience may have. This information can guide you in creating content or features that address these needs and show up for them when they Google a question about your product.

- **Social Media Listening Tools:** Tools like Brandwatch, Hootsuite, or Mention enable you to monitor conversations and mentions of specific keywords or topics across social media platforms. You can identify common pain points and areas where your product can offer a solution by tracking discussions related to existing digital products or industry trends.

Step 2: Validating the Idea

Validating your digital product idea involves testing its viability and market acceptance before investing significant resources into development. Key steps in the validation process include:

- Creating a minimum viable product (MVP) that demonstrates core functionality and value proposition. A minimum viable product is a version of a product with just enough features to be usable by early customers, who can then provide feedback for future product development.

- Testing the MVP with a small audience to gather feedback and validate market demand. You can then iterate the product and repeat the process until you have an amazing product that meets your customer's needs.

Step 3: Creating the Product

Once your digital product idea has been validated, it's time to bring it to life. This involves:

- Planning the content or features of your digital product to align with customer needs and preferences. The creative process can also be outsourced to experts. You can use sites like Upwork, Fiverr, and Contra to find writers, course creators, and graphic designers to help you. Whether you're creating an eBook or digital art, these platforms have a wide range of freelancers that are also great for outsourcing.

- Developing the product using appropriate tools or software, ensuring usability, functionality, and scalability. This may require some outsourcing. In any case, there are countless ways to create your digital product with the resources you have available. If you're creating an eBook, you can use Amazon KDP or IngramSpark as self-publishing platforms. If you're creating an online course, you can use Teachable, Coursera, and many other platforms that almost always let you join for free.

Step 4: Launch and Iterate

Launching your digital product to the market is just the beginning of its journey. Continuously collecting feedback and making iterative improvements based on customer input is essential for long-term success. Steps in this phase include:

- Launching the product to the market in a strategic and coordinated manner, leveraging pre-launch promotions and partnerships.

- Collecting feedback from customers through surveys, reviews, and support channels.

- Iterating on the product based on customer feedback and market trends to enhance its value and relevance over time.

But where can you launch your digital product?
Let's take a look at some of the most popular platforms.

- **eBooks:** Books sold in electronic formats are often distributed through platforms like Amazon Kindle Direct Publishing (KDP), Smashwords, and Draft2Digital. Nowadays, there are almost endless platforms to choose from, but the most popular ones like Amazon and IngramSpark are worth looking into if you want a wider audience. However, you can always sell on multiple. There are also lots of eBook creation tools like Scrivener, Calibre, and Vellum that will help you write and format the book. Tools like Brush, Canva, and Adobe can help you design the book as well. Canva is great for beginners and has a free version with plenty of features. Adobe is used more often by professionals who may be hired to handle the creative work.

- **Online courses:** Online courses provide educational content delivered over the internet. Course platforms like Thinkific, Coursera, Udemy, and Teachable allow you to create accounts for free and automatically distribute content to those who buy video creation tools like ScreenFlow, OBS Studio, and Camtasia, which can help you create videos to accompany the course.

- **Design templates:** Template creation tools like Canva, Adobe Illustrator, and Adobe Photoshop can help you create the design and make it available for download once someone purchases a template.

You can sell them through online platforms like Etsy, Showit, and other website platforms that allow people to buy directly. Etsy is a great place to start for a beginner, but Showit is better if you plan on building a website and running ads.

- **Digital artwork:** These businesses often operate on art marketplaces like Etsy, Society6, Redbubble, and ArtStation. Graphic design software like Canva and Adobe Illustrator may also be useful in creating artwork. Licensing platforms like iStock and Shutterstock are also necessary to start your digital artwork business.

- **Audio content:** To produce and distribute digital audio files as your business, you need to find a hosting platform that fits what you're selling. For instance, if you're hosting a podcast, you could look into podcast hosting platforms like Podbean, Anchor, Libsyn, or Buzzsprout, all of which offer free plans. If you're distributing music, you could look into platforms like CD Baby, TuneCore, or DistroKid. While it's uncommon for these platforms to be free, it's necessary to sign up with them to distribute music. You may also be interested in using audio editing software to perfect your files before sending them out to the public. Some of the most popular editing platforms include Audacity, Adobe Audition, and GarageBand, many of which offer free plans. However, if you outsource the editing portion, which is often recommended, the expert will already be using these tools.

Step 5: Marketing and Promotion

Building awareness and generating interest in your digital product requires strategic marketing and promotion efforts. Key activities include:

- **Paid Search Advertising:** Utilize platforms like Google Ads to bid on keywords related to your digital product. This ensures your product appears prominently in search engine results when users search for relevant terms. You can use plenty of free tools like Ubersuggest and Google Keyword Planner to figure out what your ideal customers are searching for when they seek out the solution you provide

- **Social Media Advertising:** Platforms such as Facebook, Instagram, and LinkedIn offer tons of advertising capabilities to target specific demographics based on interests, behaviors, and demographics. Sponsored posts, carousel ads, and video ads can display your digital product to a highly targeted audience.

- **Display Advertising:** Display ads can be placed on relevant websites and platforms through networks like Google Display Network or directly with publishers. These ads can be static banners, animated graphics, or interactive rich media ads, effectively capturing the attention of potential customers as they browse the web.

- **Influencer Marketing:** Partnering with influencers in your niche can amplify your reach and credibility. Influencers can create sponsored content, reviews, or endorsements to introduce your digital product to their engaged audience, driving traffic and conversions.

- **Building a Website or Landing Page:** A dedicated website or landing page serves as the central hub for your digital product, providing comprehensive information, testimonials, and a seamless purchasing or subscription process. It should be optimized for search engines and designed to convert visitors into customers or leads. This should be complete before running any ads. You can use Squarespace, Wix, Showit, and many other platforms to create a site or landing page that can easily be optimized for Google.

- **Content Marketing:** Create valuable, informative content related to your digital product niche to attract and engage your target audience. This can take various forms, including blog posts, articles, videos, infographics, podcasts, and webinars. Distribute this content through your website, social media channels, and email newsletters to establish authority as a brand and drive traffic to your site.

- **Online Communities and Forums:** Participate in online communities, forums, and discussion groups relevant to your niche. Provide valuable insights, answer questions, and establish yourself as a knowledgeable authority. Avoid obvious promotional tactics and focus on building trust within the community. Gradually introduce your digital product when relevant, respecting community guidelines and etiquette. The goal here shouldn't be to promote your product, it should be to provide value, which will position your brand as an authority on the topic related to your product.

Of course, be sure to regularly monitor and analyze your marketing efforts to optimize performance. As we mentioned earlier, the initial business-building activities will demand lots of your time, but ongoing marketing like graphic design, social media posts, and running ads can often be outsourced.

By following these steps, you can increase the likelihood of creating a viable and successful product that meets the needs of your target audience and drives sustainable growth.

As we've discussed in this chapter, understanding the nuances of digital product development—from idea generation to market research—is essential for navigating this landscape effectively. When. you embrace a systematic approach to product development, you can mitigate risks, capitalize on emerging trends, and position your digital product for long-term success. With diligence, creativity, and a willingness to adapt, you can maximize your chances of creating a viable and profitable digital product that resonates with your target audience for decades to come.

66

"**Customer service** should not be a department. It should be the **entire** company."

– TONY HSIEH –

Chapter 6: Business Idea #2

Service Arbitrage

When it comes to online entrepreneurship, opportunities can often seem both abundant and overwhelming. Yet, there exists a business model that thrives on simplicity and scalability. This model, known as Services Arbitrage, involves acting as a middle person in transactions delivering various services, thereby generating revenue through strategic markup.

To understand Services Arbitrage and its potential for success as a business, let's examine the story of Yaro Starak, the founder of InboxDone.com, a thriving business built upon this exact model.

Yaro's journey into the realm of online business began with BetterEdit.com, a platform connecting students with editors for thesis and essay papers. Through this, he not only crafted a full-time income stream but also honed his understanding of the Services Arbitrage model since he was the middleman between the people buying and delivering the actual services.

In 2017, Yaro seized the opportunity to bring his vision further with InboxDone.com. Leveraging the principles of Services Arbitrage, InboxDone.com rapidly burgeoned into a six-figure revenue-generating entity within its first year, crossing the million-dollar mark soon after. InboxDone.com was like BetterEdit.com and offered email management services. Today, Service Arbitrage businesses can offer a wide range of services like podcast editing, audio production, and even legal services.

The way that Yaro was able to capitalize on this business model not once, but twice in such a short period of time, shows how the model is a strong business idea. Online entrepreneurship isn't solely reserved for those with specialized expertise or extensive resources. It's for aspiring entrepreneurs like us who are willing to understand supply and demand, connectivity, and strategic marketing.

What Is Service Arbitrage?

As mentioned, Services Arbitrage revolves around profiting as an intermediary by facilitating service transactions. Imagine being the bridge between clients seeking a particular service and skilled professionals capable of delivering it. Your role entails sourcing clients, connecting them with service providers, and earning a markup on the transaction.

Yaro's venture, BetterEdit.com, is the perfect example. Students in need of editing services were connected with skilled editors through the platform. BetterEdit.com handled the marketing and client acquisition while outsourcing the editing tasks to contractors, thus pocketing the difference between what clients paid and what editors were compensated.

From copywriting and video editing to graphic design and legal services, the opportunities are endless with this business model. Since you're the intermediary and not always the person delivering the services, there's also loads of room to get creative in marketing and building your business (more on this later).

Major companies like Airbnb and Uber operate on the Services Arbitrage model, connecting clients needing transportation services with contract drivers or those who need a place to stay with homeowners. There are many ways that you can not only be successful with this model but also make money on a grand scale.

Services Arbitrage presents a pathway to entrepreneurial success marked by minimal overhead, scalable revenue streams, and the potential for exponential growth. As we delve deeper into its intricacies, you'll discover how to leverage this model to carve your niche in the digital marketplace.

Scoring the Service Arbitrage Business

Let's evaluate the Service Arbitrage business idea on a scale of 1-5 in terms of the time and money to get started and the effort it will require to maintain it.

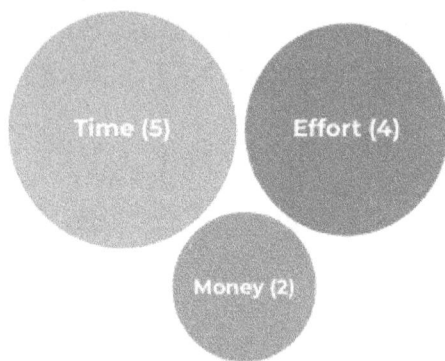

Time: 5/5

Most of the effort regarding this business model is in the initial setup. If you're hoping to start a service arbitrage business, you need to make sure you have enough time to build the entire thing from the ground up. The time effort will be spent on finding and securing the service providers you will use; this will include agreeing terms of the relationship and a price structure. Additional effort will then be required to develop your brand and market your services.

Money: 2/5

Startup costs when it comes to Service Arbitrage businesses are low. This business type primarily depends on time rather than significant financial resources. You don't need to buy any equipment or employ any professionals. The essence and beauty of this business idea is that everything is outsourced. You can also generate leads without substantial financial investment. The main costs will be associated with website creation and marketing. Financial returns may also take time to materialize in the initial phases.

Effort: 4/5

You will have the opportunity to outsource tasks and scale the business with relative ease. You'll also have great potential for leveraging existing skills in communication and marketing. However, the ongoing effort may be higher, particularly in managing client relationships and overseeing service delivery. As Tony Hsieh once said, "Customer service should not be a department. It should be the entire company." Skill in delegation and customer management is essential for long-term sustainability.

Start a Service Arbitrage Business

- Step 1: Identify Your Niche and Target Audience
- Step 2: Build a Network of Service Providers
- Step 3: Establish an Online Presence
- Step 4: Implement Efficient Operations and Management Systems
- Step 5: Provide Excellent Customer Service

Step 1: Identify Your Niche and Target Audience

This business model starts with finding your space in the marketplace:

- Utilizing online platforms like Upwork, Freelancer, and Fiverr is a fantastic starting point. Go on these platforms and see which services people are looking for. These platforms act as the middleman between those who supply and need the services, so identifying how it works can help you brainstorm ideas for the services you could help provide. Then, you can start to identify your own niche and target audience.

- Platforms like SEMrush, Ahrefs, or Google Keyword Planner can also provide data on the volume of searches related to different services within your potential niche. Look for keywords with high search volume but low competition to identify underserved areas. This will help you utilize these keywords and come up when people search for your services. For instance, if you go on Fiverr and notice that many people are searching for a graphic designer, you can offer these services through your own business. To attract these potential customers, you can conduct further research to find out what questions they are searching for when it comes to those services. Then, you can create answers on your website to target these specific inquiries and increase your chances of being seen by those potential customers.

- Conducting surveys among your target audience or within relevant online communities can provide even more direct feedback on their pain points, needs, and preferences. Tools like SurveyMonkey, Google Forms, or Typeform can help you create and distribute surveys efficiently, which is a great way to conduct more in-depth market research.

- You can also explore industry-specific reports, journals, and publications to gain a deeper understanding of market trends, challenges, and opportunities. Websites like Statista, IBISWorld, or industry-specific associations often provide valuable data and insights on how your niche is growing (or not!).

- Once you have a niche or two in mind, it's time to establish your own competitive edge or unique selling point. Tools like SpyFu, SimilarWeb, or Moz can help you analyze your competitors' strategies, pricing, and customer base. Identify gaps in their service offerings or areas where you can differentiate yourself to carve out your niche.

- Monitor conversations and trends related to your potential niche on social media platforms using tools like Hootsuite, Sprout Social, or Mention. Pay attention to what your target audience is discussing, their pain points, and the solutions they seek. This shouldn't be a one-time thing—continue doing this to continually optimize your own business.

Similarly, analyze search trends over time using Google Trends to identify rising interests and potential opportunities within your niche. This can help you stay ahead of emerging trends and adjust your service offerings accordingly. Once you have all that information, it's time to start building your business. Keep in mind that market research is heavy in the beginning but must continue to be conducted throughout the entire lifetime of your business to maintain your competitive advantage.

Step 2: Build a Network of Service Providers

Collaborating with professionals who will provide the best services is essential, and here's how you can achieve it:

- Leverage online platforms and industry forums to connect with skilled professionals in your chosen niche. This is also where freelancer platforms like

Upwork and Fiverr may come into play. You can also get recommendations from others who have worked with the experts you're looking for.

- Utilize platforms like LinkedIn to search for and connect with professionals in your niche. Send personalized messages introducing yourself and expressing your interest in collaborating. LinkedIn also offers features like ProFinder, which can help you find freelancers based on your specific requirements.

- Use tools like DocuSign or HelloSign to streamline the negotiation process and formalize agreements with your service providers. Clearly outline pricing, payment terms, deliverables, timelines, and any other relevant terms to ensure mutual understanding and agreement.

- As such, you should also establish clear communication channels with your service providers from the outset. Utilize project management tools like Trello, Asana, or Slack to facilitate communication, share updates, and track progress efficiently. Clearly define expectations, preferred communication methods, and response times to avoid misunderstandings and ensure smooth collaboration.

- Continuously nurture these relationships, provide feedback, and maintain transparency to foster long-term partnerships and keep your providers for years to come.

Step 3: Establish an Online Presence

- An online presence for your business is an essential platform for you to reach your customers effectively. This involves the following steps: First, invest in a professionally designed website to showcase your services, portfolio, and customer reviews. Ensure that your website is user-friendly, visually appealing, and optimized for both desktop and mobile devices. Platforms like WordPress, Wix, or Squarespace offer easy-to-use tools for creating and customizing your website. You can also outsource this work to freelancers on platforms designed for that purpose.

- Optimize your website for search engines to improve its visibility and attract organic traffic. Conduct keyword research to identify relevant search terms related to your services and integrate them into your website content, meta tags, and headings. Focus on creating high-quality, relevant content that addresses the needs of your target audience and earns backlinks from reputable websites.

- Create profiles on relevant social media platforms such as LinkedIn, Facebook, or Instagram to connect with your audience and highlight your providers' areas of expertise. Share valuable content, industry insights, and updates about your services to engage with potential buyers. Utilize social media management tools like Buffer, Hootsuite, or Sprout Social to schedule posts and monitor engagement effectively. This task can also be outsourced!

- Develop a content marketing strategy to establish thought leadership in your niche and attract potential clients. Create blog posts, articles, case studies, or videos demonstrating your expertise and provide value to your target audience. Publish content regularly on your website and share it across your social media channels to drive traffic and generate leads.

- You can also use online advertising platforms like Google Ads, Facebook Ads, or LinkedIn Ads to reach potential clients and promote your services. Set clear objectives, target specific demographics or industries, and create compelling ad creatives that highlight the benefits of working with your business. Monitor your ad performance regularly and adjust your campaigns based on results to maximize ROI. You can outsource this to agencies that optimize and run ads as well.

- Build an email list of prospective clients and existing customers and implement email marketing campaigns to nurture leads and stay top-of-mind. Send personalized emails with valuable content, special offers, or updates about your services to engage with your audience and encourage them to take action. Use email marketing platforms like Mailchimp, Constant Contact, or ConvertKit to automate and track your email campaigns effectively.

- Collaborate with other professionals, influencers, or complementary businesses in your niche to expand your reach and attract new clients. Participate in online networking events, webinars, or collaborative projects to build relationships and leverage each other's audiences.

Step 4: Implement Efficient Operations and Management Systems

Efficient operations and management systems are essential for running a successful service arbitrage business. Here are some activities to consider:

- Be sure to develop standardized workflows for your business processes, from client onboarding to project delivery and invoicing. Clearly outline the steps involved in each process and ensure consistency across projects. Tools like Lucidchart, Trello, or Microsoft Visio can help you map out workflows and identify areas for optimization while keeping everything in one place.

- You can also use project management tools like Asana, Trello, or Basecamp to organize tasks, assign responsibilities, and track project progress. You can create project timelines, set deadlines, and collaborate with your team and service providers in real time. These tools facilitate communication, file sharing, and task management, ensuring that projects are completed efficiently and on schedule.

- With these tools, you can delegate tasks effectively to your team and service providers based on their skills and expertise. Clearly communicate expectations, deadlines, and deliverables to avoid misunderstandings and ensure accountability. Regularly check in with team members to provide support, address challenges, and ensure that projects stay on track.

- Integrate pricing and financial management tools to accurately track expenses, revenue, and profit margins. Use accounting software like QuickBooks, Xero, or FreshBooks to manage invoicing, expenses, and financial reporting. Monitor your cash flow, track project profitability, and make data-driven decisions to optimize your business operations.

- As far as actual workflows, you can explore automation platforms like Zapier, IFTTT, or Microsoft Power Automate to automate workflows, integrate applications, and eliminate manual data entry.

Automate email notifications, data syncing, and task reminders to save time on your end and reduce errors. This can also be done through CRM (customer relationship management). CRM is a set of integrated, data-driven software solutions that help manage, track, and store information related to your company's current and potential customers. Implement a CRM system to manage client relationships, track interactions, and streamline customer support processes. Choose a CRM platform like Salesforce, HubSpot, or Zoho CRM that aligns with your business needs and scale. Centralize client information, track communication history, and personalize your interactions to enhance customer satisfaction and retention. You can also communicate your standard operating procedures while onboarding someone.

Step 5: Provide Excellent Customer Service

As Teddy Roosevelt once said, "People do not care how much you know until they know how much you care," and this couldn't be truer when it comes to the service arbitrage business model. Consider the following to achieve great customer satisfaction:

- To deliver customer satisfaction and outstanding service, prioritize personalized communication with your clients to show that you genuinely care about their needs and preferences. Address clients by their names, tailor your communication style to their preferences, and provide regular updates on project progress. Use tools like personalized email templates, CRM systems, and client management platforms to manage interactions efficiently and train your service providers on how to communicate.

- Respect your clients' time by delivering services promptly and meeting agreed-upon deadlines. Set realistic timelines for project delivery, communicate any potential delays proactively, and strive to exceed expectations whenever possible. Use project management tools and workflow automation to streamline processes and ensure timely delivery of services, which can usually all be done through one CRM.

- Go above and beyond by offering value-added services that enhance the client experience and provide additional value. Identify opportunities to anticipate and fulfill your clients' needs before they even ask. This could include offering complimentary consultations, educational resources, or personalized recommendations tailored to their business goals. This is also a great way to offer value-based services that don't rely so much on time.

- Actively solicit feedback from your clients at various touchpoints throughout the engagement process. Use surveys, feedback forms, or one-on-one conversations to gather input on their experience, satisfaction levels, and areas for improvement. Analyze feedback systematically and use it to identify trends, refine your processes, and enhance your service offerings based on ongoing needs.

- As such, it's best to adopt a culture of continuous improvement within your business, where feedback is valued, and lessons learned are used to drive positive change. Regularly evaluate your customer service processes, performance metrics, and client satisfaction levels. Identify areas for optimization, invest in training and development opportunities for your team, and strive to raise the bar for customer service excellence.

Ultimately, service arbitrage businesses are great for those who want to act as the middleman between service providers and buyers instead of providing the services themselves. It's also an ideal business model for those who enjoy running and overseeing a business as opposed to interacting 1-on-1 with clients. As a service arbitrage business owner, you'll likely spend most of your time overseeing the business operations and marketing the business as opposed to providing services like other business owners.

By prioritizing customer satisfaction, embracing innovation, and cultivating a culture of continuous improvement, you can transform satisfied customers into raving fans and build a service arbitrage business that continually evolves and stands the test of time.

66

"The **future** of retail is e-commerce. Customers **demand** it, and the trend shows no sign of **slowing** down."

– ELON MUSK –

Chapter 7: Business Idea #3

Dropshipping

To truly understand the potential a dropshipping business model holds, let's dive into the story of Irwin Dominguez, a successful dropshipper who went from zero to $1,000,000 in just eight months. Inspired by a friend's success, Irwin was inspired to start his own online store by opening a Shopify account using Oberlo to ship items directly to his customers.

He made his first sale through Facebook ads, one of the most common ways for Shopify stores to advertise. Although the cost of advertising ate through a lot of his money, according to him, it ended up being one of the most ROI-positive investments of his career since it jump-started the store.

Now, on his best day, Irwin pulls in up to $30,000. He's currently averaging around $10,000 per day in profit. But how did he get here? He attributes his success to two pro tips that he followed. First, validate your product idea before jumping in. Instead of dealing in large quantities, make sure you can generate those first few sales. When you recognize the potential, you can start to scale. Second, be prepared when those floodgates open and the sales start coming in. Once you find a product that has potential, put the necessary mechanisms in place that allow your store to run seamlessly.

What Is Dropshipping?

Dropshipping is an e-commerce business model that's gained tons of momentum in recent years, especially among aspiring entrepreneurs. Dropshipping involves selling products, or sometimes just one product, from a single store to customers without the need to store inventory. Instead, when a customer purchases from your online store, you simply forward the order to a third-party supplier, who then ships the product directly to the customer.

In a way, dropshipping is like the service arbitrage business model we discussed in the last chapter, as the dropshipper acts as the middleman between the buyer and the person who ships out the product. The main difference is that dropshipping involves providing products rather than services. The dropshipper does the marketing and promotion of the product while making a profit, without having to handle packaging, shipping, storing, or investing in inventory.

One popular alternative to dropshipping is Fulfillment by Amazon (FBA). With Amazon FBA, sellers send their products to Amazon's fulfillment centers, where the items are stored, packed, and shipped to customers when orders are placed. This means sellers can leverage Amazon's vast infrastructure and logistics network, allowing for faster shipping times and often lower shipping costs.

One of the key advantages of Amazon FBA is its reputation for reliability. Amazon has built a trusted brand known for its fast and efficient delivery, which can help sellers establish credibility and trust with customers. Additionally, by outsourcing fulfillment to Amazon, sellers can focus more on other aspects of their business, such as marketing and product development, rather than dealing with the complexities of inventory management and shipping logistics.

These can all still be achieved with dropshipping as well. Many times, dropshippers have Shopify stores and outsource the shipping to Alibaba, AliExpress, or other platforms that are just as reliable as Amazon. With that said, if you're considering Amazon FBA, this chapter will likely not only help you make that choice but also help you understand the overall benefits of being the middleman.

Scoring the Dropshipping Business

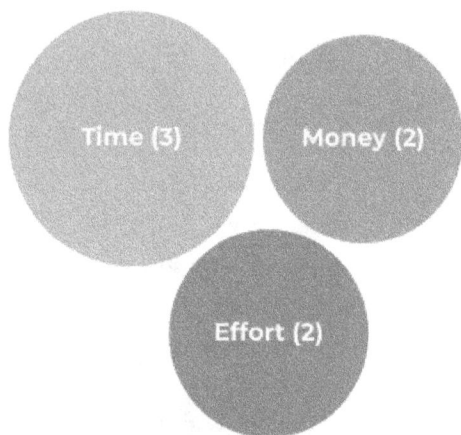

Time (3)

Money (2)

Effort (2)

Time: 3/5

Setting up a dropshipping business requires an initial time investment. This involves building your online store, sourcing suppliers, and setting up marketing campaigns. Another primary focus is selecting niches and products that you will be dropshipping, which is key to achieving success and requires significant initial effort. However, many tasks can be outsourced later, and we'll explore this further in this chapter.

Money: 2/5

Dropshipping boasts low startup costs compared to traditional brick-and-mortar businesses. Since the entire operation is online and there's no need to invest in inventory upfront, you can launch your online store even with minimal capital to begin with. The exception is Amazon FBA, whereby some investment in inventory would be required.

Effort: 2/5

One of the key appeals of dropshipping is its potential for remote operation and flexibility. Dropshippers can manage their businesses from anywhere with an internet connection, making it a great business model for those who want work-life balance and more passive income. The ongoing effort required to maintain a dropshipping store is low, particularly once streamlined processes are in place and regular tasks are outsourced.

Steps to Starting a Dropshipping Business

- Step 1: Choose Your Niche
- Step 2: Set Up Your Store
- Step 3: Find Reliable Suppliers
- Step 4: Optimize for Sales
- Step 5: Provide Excellent Ongoing Customer Service
- Step 6: Delegate Customer Service Tasks to a Virtual Assistant

Step 1: Choose Your Niche

Identifying the right niche is crucial for dropshipping success. Begin by researching trending products that are in high demand. You can start by using tools such as:

- **Google Trends:** Analyze search volume trends to identify products on the rise. Use filters to narrow down your search by time period. The more recent the product has been trending, the better!

- **Amazon Best Sellers:** Explore the top-selling products across various categories to uncover lucrative opportunities. Pay attention to high-demand niche markets—these are your best bets.

- **Shopify's Oberlo:** Leverage Oberlo's product research feature to discover trending items with high profit potential. Filter products based on factors like order volume and shipping options. This step is necessary if you plan on starting a Shopify store.

Step 2: Set Up Your Store

Creating a high-converting and visually appealing online store is essential for attracting customers and driving sales. The first step is to choose a platform. Consider ease of use, customization options, and integration with dropshipping plugins. Popular platforms include:

- **Shopify:** Known for its user-friendly interface and extensive app ecosystem, Shopify is by far the most popular platform for dropshipping businesses. It's also beginner-friendly, and if you plan on having a mentor, they will likely already be familiar with this platform and all the others that can be integrated into it as well.

- **WooCommerce:** WooCommerce is ideal for WordPress users seeking flexibility and control over their online store. You can manage your own security, backups, and hosting, which gives you autonomy but isn't the best option if you're a beginner to these platforms.

The next part of setting up your online store is establishing your domain name. Choose a memorable and relevant domain name that reflects your brand and resonates with your target audience, even if it's just a one-word brand name. Two of the most successful dropshipping stores include Warmly and Bluecrate—simple but memorable and catchy brand names.

Once you set up your brand name and URL, it's time to start plugging things into your store to streamline product importation and order fulfillment. Leverage tools like:

- **Oberlo:** Specifically designed for Shopify, Oberlo offers a vast selection of products sourced from

AliExpress. It simplifies product importing and order management.

- **AliExpress:** While not a plugin itself, AliExpress is a popular marketplace for sourcing dropshipping products. Many e-commerce platforms offer integrations or extensions to facilitate product importation from AliExpress.

Step 3: Find Reliable Suppliers

Partnering with trustworthy suppliers ensures you consistently deliver high-quality products to your customers. Remember, you're just the middleman, so finding someone you trust to ship out products that arrive in great shape is a must. Here's how to find and vet reliable suppliers:

- **Do Your Research:** Look for suppliers with a track record of reliability and positive reviews from other dropshippers. Consider product quality, shipping times, and customer service.

- **Establish Clear Communication Channels:** Communicate your expectations regarding product quality, shipping procedures, and order fulfillment deadlines. Regular communication helps build trust and ensures any issues are addressed promptly, which contributes to your store's customer service.

- **Define Terms and Agreements:** Define clear terms and agreements with your suppliers to protect your business interests. Negotiate pricing, minimum order quantities, and payment terms upfront. Formalize agreements through contracts or written agreements to avoid misunderstandings later.

But where can you connect with suppliers? Consider these popular platforms:

- **Alibaba:** Alibaba is a leading online marketplace connecting businesses with suppliers worldwide. You can use Alibaba's search filters and supplier verification tools to find reliable partners.

- **SaleHoo:** An online directory of wholesalers, dropshippers, and manufacturers, SaleHoo provides detailed supplier profiles and user reviews to help you make informed decisions.

- **Trade shows and exhibitions:** Attend industry trade shows and exhibitions to meet potential suppliers and establish direct relationships. These events offer opportunities to discuss terms face-to-face and inspect product samples. This is a fantastic way to go once your store is already gaining momentum.

Step 4: Optimize for Sales

Maximizing sales requires optimizing your online store and implementing effective marketing efforts. Here's how to optimize your dropshipping business for sales:

- **Create Product Descriptions and Images:** Craft compelling product descriptions highlighting key features and benefits of what you're selling. Use high-quality images to showcase products from different angles. Consider hiring a professional copywriter and photographer to ensure your product listings stand out, especially if it's a popular product. In this case, branding is crucial—make sure you establish an entire brand identity that remains consistent across your store. This includes a brand voice, color scheme, and logos.

- **Invest in Web Design and Development:** Invest in professional web design and development to create a visually appealing and user-friendly online store. A well-designed website enhances credibility and encourages visitors to explore your products further. This is also a terrific way to establish those branding aspects.

- **Prioritize SEO Optimization:** Improve your website's visibility on search engines through search engine optimization. Conduct keyword research to identify relevant search terms and incorporate them into your website's content, meta tags, and product descriptions. Optimize site speed, mobile responsiveness, and user experience to rank higher in search results. You can also outsource this to an SEO specialist or find a copywriter specializing in keyword-rich copy.

- **Advertising on Facebook and Google Ads:** Use Facebook Ads and Google Ads to reach your target audience and drive traffic to your online store. Facebook Ads are highly effective for dropshipping businesses due to their advanced targeting options and visual ad formats.

Step 5: Provide Excellent Ongoing Customer Service

Delivering exceptional customer service is vital for building trust and loyalty with your customers. Here's how to ensure top-notch customer support for your dropshipping business:

- **Set Up Timely Responses:** Set up a system for promptly addressing customer inquiries and concerns. Use customer service management tools like Help Scout, Zendesk, or Freshdesk to manage incoming messages efficiently. Consider automating responses to common queries using chatbots or canned responses. Delegate customer service tasks to trained staff members to ensure timely resolution of issues. This is a fantastic opportunity to hire a virtual assistant if you can't automate all responses but still don't want to reply to all the customers on your own once your store begins to grow.

- **Offer Hassle-Free Returns and Refunds:** Offer a hassle-free returns and refunds policy to instill confidence in your customers. Clearly communicate your return policy on your website and ensure that the process is simple and straightforward.

- **Establish Standard Operating Procedures (SOPs):** Establish SOPs for your customer service processes to maintain consistency and efficiency. Document step-by-step guidelines for handling various scenarios, including order inquiries, returns, and refunds. Train your customer service team on these SOPs to ensure adherence to best practices and ensure your customers get a branded experience the whole way through.

Step 6: Delegate Customer Service Tasks to a Virtual Assistant

As your dropshipping business grows, managing customer inquiries and support can become increasingly time-consuming, and one of the main benefits of having a dropshipping business is that it doesn't have to take up lots of your time. Hiring a virtual assistant (VA) can alleviate this workload. When hiring a VA for your dropshipping business, consider the following steps:

- **Define Roles and Responsibilities:** Clearly outline the tasks and responsibilities you want your virtual assistant to handle. This may include responding to customer inquiries, processing returns and refunds, managing order fulfillment, and updating product listings. Make it known that these tasks need to be done in the job post when you start hiring.

- **Look for Relevant Skills and Experience:** Seek candidates with experience in customer service, e-commerce, or related fields. Look for individuals with effective communication skills, attention to detail, and the ability to multitask effectively. Prior experience with platforms like Shopify, WooCommerce, or Amazon Seller Central can be advantageous.

- **Conduct Interviews:** Take the time to interview potential candidates to assess their suitability for the role, this can easily be done using Zoom or other video conferencing tools. Ask about their previous experience and familiarity with dropshipping processes. Consider conducting a trial period to evaluate their performance before making a final decision. If they have results from past clients whose dropshipping stores they've helped run, consider that a bonus.

- **Provide Training and Guidance:** Once you've hired a virtual assistant, provide comprehensive training on your dropshipping business operations and customer service protocols. Familiarize them with your SOPs, customer service management tools, and any specific requirements or expectations you have for handling customer inquiries. This will help your store grow and give you peace of mind, knowing that they know how to handle things the same way you would without needing to give your time to the business.

- **Establish Communication Channels:** Set up clear communication channels to stay in touch with your virtual assistant. Use messaging platforms like Slack or Skype for regular communication, and schedule periodic check-ins to review performance and provide feedback.

- **Monitor Performance and Provide Feedback:** Regularly monitor your virtual assistant's performance to ensure they meet expectations and deliver high-quality customer service. Provide constructive feedback and guidance as needed to help them improve and excel in their role. Initially, it may be best to have them CC you on all communication channels or simply check by logging in.

Success in dropshipping demands adaptability, perseverance, and a commitment to continuous improvement as your store grows over time. As the e-commerce landscape evolves, entrepreneurs must stay informed about emerging trends, consumer preferences, and industry best practices to remain competitive and continue selling products online.

Dropshipping is an attractive business model for entrepreneurs who value work-life balance and have experience in marketing or sales. As a middleman between the buyer and supplier, running and growing your online store as a dropshipper can be much easier than an in-person business. It offers flexibility that's great for those who value creativity in how they run their store.

66

"You don't want **everyone** to see a piece of content. You want the people who are really **excited** about the content to **see** it."

– JONAH PERETTI –

Chapter 8: Business Idea #4

Print-on-Demand

If you're wondering how profitable a print-on-demand business is, let's look at the inspiring case study of Mike Pasley, founder of Famous in Real Life, a T-shirt brand that made $700,000 within just one year of its initial launch.

As an e-commerce entrepreneur with marketing and design skills, Pasley was inspired to start his own print-on-demand t-shirt business that sold shirts with fun designs on them. But they weren't just fun designs that you could find anywhere—they were all pop culture-focused and themed in different ways. For instance, movie fans could shop for a shirt with a fictional location based on one of their favorite movies on it. The same could be done for TV shows.

The target audience? Movie and TV fans. With such a wide target audience yet such a unique concept, there's just about something for everyone when it comes to Famous in Real Life. By taking something that everyone loves, TV and movies, and utilizing pop culture in a way that hadn't been done before, Pasley invented a product that was in high-demand and couldn't be found anywhere else.

What Is Print-on-Demand?

Print-on-Demand, POD for short, refers to a printing process in which clothes, furniture, or other printed items are produced individually, on-demand, rather than through traditional large print runs. This method offers several advantages for business owners, including cost-effectiveness, reduced waste, and the ability to cater to niche markets with minimal risk.

The entire process begins when a customer places an order for a product, such as a T-shirt with a custom design. The order details are sent to the print-on-demand service provider. This includes information like the product type, size, color, and the specific design or customization requested by the customer.

The print-on-demand provider receives the order and initiates the printing and production process. For example, if it's a T-shirt, the design is printed onto a blank shirt using digital printing technology. Once the product is manufactured, it undergoes quality control to ensure it meets the required standards and meets the customer's specifications. After passing quality control, the product is packaged and prepared for shipping. This may include adding branding materials, such as stickers or thank-you notes. The packaged product is then shipped directly to the customer's address. The print-on-demand provider or a third-party logistics company can handle the shipping process.

Third-party fulfillment in the print-on-demand model often involves partnering with companies that specialize in logistics and shipping. These third-party fulfillment companies store the blank products (e.g., T-shirts, mugs, phone cases) and handle the printing, packaging, and shipping processes on behalf of the print-on-demand service provider. This allows the print-on-demand company to focus on marketing, customer service, and managing the online storefront while outsourcing the operational aspects of fulfilling orders to specialized partners. This model can be cost-effective and scalable, as the print-on-demand provider doesn't need to invest in their own manufacturing facilities or warehouse space.

In the current market, POD is becoming increasingly popular, particularly in an era where consumers increasingly demand personalized and unique products. According to Printful, the business model is experiencing an upward growth trajectory of over 32% each year!

Today, tons of key players and platforms dominate the POD market. For instance, Redbubble, known for its diverse marketplace of independent artists, allows creators to upload designs for printing on various products, from apparel to home decor. Teespring specializes in customized apparel, empowering individuals to design and sell their own clothing lines with minimal upfront costs.

Printful offers a comprehensive print-on-demand service, integrating with e-commerce platforms like Shopify and Etsy to fulfill orders on behalf of online stores. As discussed in the last chapter, there may be similarities with dropshipping, but keep in mind that print-on-demand businesses require connecting with a designer and creating unique designs, unlike dropshipping, where the supplier would already have the product ready to be shipped.

The POD industry empowers entrepreneurs to share their visions with the world and sell their creations in a more cost-effective and environmentally friendly way. From an entrepreneurial standpoint and for our purposes, the business model provides flexibility, accessibility, and limitless potential for innovation.

Scoring the Print-on-Demand Business

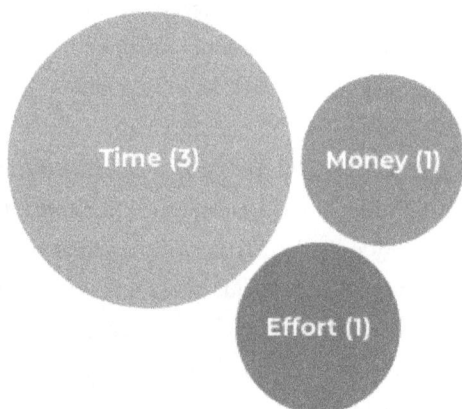

Time (3)

Money (1)

Effort (1)

Time: 3/5

Starting a print-on-demand business requires moderate setup time before you can outsource tasks. This includes coming up with your designs, establishing how you'll market them, and establishing your niche in the marketplace. We'll explore how to set up the business later in this chapter.

Money: 1/5

This business model offers low upfront costs and minimal risks, making it a financially accessible option for aspiring entrepreneurs. With no inventory requirements and the ability to outsource at a relatively low cost, the initial investment is significantly lower than other business models.

Effort: 1/5

The effort to maintain this type of business model is low and one of its most beneficial features. Once set up, the business can run itself, allowing entrepreneurs to focus on strategic growth initiatives rather than day-to-day operations.

Steps to Start a Print-on-Demand Business

- Step 1: Conduct Market Research
- Step 2: Select the Right Platform
- Step 3: Source High-Quality Products & Design
- Step 4: Set Up Your Online Store
- Step 5: Promote Your Shop
- Step 6: Automate Fulfillment & Customer Service
- Step 7: Monitor & Optimize Shop Performance

Step 1: Conduct Market Research

To effectively target your audience and stand out in the space, conduct detailed market research focused on identifying specific design themes, styles, and product selection within your chosen niche. Use Google Trends, Amazon Best Sellers, and social media analytics to pinpoint emerging design trends and popular product categories. Determine which types of products, whether apparel, home furnishings, or niche-specific items, resonate most with your target demographic, considering both demand and production capabilities. Explore different aesthetics, such as modern, vintage, quirky, or minimalist, and align them with your brand and audience preferences. Validate your choices through audience engagement by using social media polls, surveys, or focus groups to gather feedback and ensure market resonance. This research will inform your product selection, design strategy, and marketing approach, laying the foundation for a successful business.

Step 2: Select the Right Platform

Choose the right e-commerce platform for your POD business based on features, integrations, and target audience. Each platform offers unique capabilities tailored to POD businesses, so consider the following platforms and what each has to offer when making your selection:

- **Shopify:** A popular choice for POD businesses due to its robust features, customizable themes, and seamless integrations with POD fulfillment services like Printful and Printify. With Shopify, you can easily create a professional online store, manage inventory, process orders, and leverage marketing tools to drive sales. Its extensive app ecosystem allows you to enhance functionality and automate tasks, making it ideal for scaling your business.

- **Etsy:** A leading marketplace for handmade and vintage goods, making it an excellent platform for selling unique products to a niche audience. With Etsy, you can create a storefront to showcase your POD creations, benefit from built-in traffic and discoverability, and engage with a community of like-minded shoppers. Additionally, Etsy's integration with Printful enables seamless order fulfillment, simplifying the selling process.

- **Amazon Merch:** Amazon Merch is a POD service specifically designed for selling custom apparel and merchandise on the Amazon marketplace. As one of the largest e-commerce platforms globally, Amazon Merch offers unparalleled reach and visibility, allowing POD businesses to tap into a massive customer base. With Amazon Merch, you can create and list your POD products directly on Amazon, leverage its powerful search and recommendation algorithms, and benefit from Prime shipping options to attract and retain customers.

Step 3: Source High-Quality Products & Design

Sourcing high-quality designs is essential to attract customers and differentiate your products in the market. Here are some ways you can efficiently source and create designs for your POD business:

- **Use Graphic Design Software:** When necessary, use professional graphic design software such as Adobe Photoshop and Illustrator to create custom designs. These tools offer advanced features and flexibility, allowing you to produce stunning designs for your POD products without outsourcing the design aspect. Invest time in mastering these platforms to craft unique and visually appealing artwork that resonates with your customers.

- **Use Freelancer Platforms:** If you prefer to outsource design tasks or need assistance with specialized projects, consider hiring freelance designers on platforms like Upwork, Contra, and Fiverr. These platforms connect you with talented designers from around the world, allowing you to find the right fit for your project based on skills, experience, and budget. Whether you need logo design, illustration, or product mockups, freelancers can provide customized solutions to bring your creative vision to life before you start making sales.

Step 4: Set Up Your Online Store

Once you've chosen the right platform, it's time to set up your online store:

- **Choose the Right Template:** Start by selecting a template or theme provided by your chosen platform that aligns with your brand identity and target audience. Look for templates that offer clean layouts, intuitive navigation, and customizable design elements to create a professional and cohesive look for your store that aligns with your brand.

- **Customize Your Design:** Personalize your store's design to reflect your brand personality and connect with your customers. Use your brand colors, logo, and imagery consistently throughout your store to establish brand recognition and gain trust with visitors. Optimize your design for mobile responsiveness to ensure a seamless shopping experience on all devices. If you hire a web designer, they should be able to do this part for you.

- **Highlight Your Best-Selling Products:** Showcase your best-selling and most popular POD products prominently on your homepage and category pages to capture the attention of visitors and encourage them to browse further.

- **Optimize Product Pages:** Create informative and engaging product pages that provide detailed descriptions, sizing information if needed, and product specifications. Use high-resolution images and multiple angles to showcase your products effectively, allowing customers to visualize their purchase and alleviate any hesitations. Incorporate customer reviews and testimonials to build credibility and reassure potential buyers.

- **Implement Clear Call-to-Action (CTA) Buttons:** Use clear call-to-actions throughout your store to guide visitors toward desired actions, such as adding products to the cart, completing checkout, or signing up for newsletters. Use actionable language and contrasting colors to make CTAs stand out and encourage conversions.

- **Offer a Seamless Checkout Experience:** Streamline the checkout process to minimize friction and maximize conversions. To accommodate diverse customer preferences, provide multiple payment options, including credit cards, PayPal, and alternative payment methods. Implement guest checkout functionality to simplify the purchase process for first-time buyers and reduce cart abandonment rates.

Step 5: Promote Your Shop

To drive traffic and sales to your business, it's crucial to implement effective marketing and promotion strategies leveraging various channels and tactics. Here are a few ways you can promote your POD products:

- **Social Media Marketing:** Establish a strong presence on popular social media platforms such as Instagram, Pinterest, Facebook, and TikTok to connect with your target audience and showcase your products. Share images and videos of your products, engage with followers, and leverage hashtags and geotags to increase visibility. Utilize Instagram Stories, Facebook Live, and Pinterest Pins to showcase new arrivals, behind-the-scenes content, and customer testimonials.

- **Email Marketing Campaigns:** Build and nurture relationships with your audience through targeted email marketing campaigns using platforms like Mailchimp, Constant Contact, or Klaviyo. Segment your email list based on customer preferences, purchase history, and engagement levels, and tailor your messages and offers accordingly. Send personalized product recommendations, exclusive discounts, and seasonal promotions to incentivize repeat purchases and drive conversions. Implement automated email sequences, such as welcome emails, abandoned cart reminders, and post-purchase follow-ups, to engage customers at every stage of the buyer's journey and maximize lifetime value.

- **Influencer Collaborations:** Partner with influencers, bloggers, and content creators in your niche to amplify your reach and credibility within your target audience. Identify influencers whose values and aesthetics align with your brand and reach out to them with personalized collaboration proposals. Offer them free products or affiliate commissions in exchange for authentic reviews, sponsored posts, or product placements on their social media channels and blogs. Encourage influencers to share user-generated content featuring your products, engage with their followers, and drive traffic to your online store through affiliate links or discount codes.

- **Run Advertising Campaigns:** Use paid advertising platforms like Google Ads, Facebook Ads, Instagram Ads, and Pinterest Ads to drive targeted traffic to your print-on-demand store. Create visually appealing ads showcasing your products and use audience targeting options to reach users based on demographics, interests, and online behavior. Experiment with different ad formats, such as image ads, carousel ads, and video ads, and optimize your campaigns based on key performance indicators like click-through rates, conversion rates, and return on ad spend. Implement retargeting campaigns to re-engage users who have previously visited your website but didn't make a purchase. Lastly, use A/B testing (also known as split testing or bucket testing) to compare two versions and determine which one performs better). This will help you refine your ad copy, visuals, and targeting parameters for optimal results.

Step 6: Automate Fulfillment & Customer Service

Efficient fulfillment and customer service are critical aspects of running a successful POD business. Here's how you can effectively manage fulfillment and customer service using integrated services and customer support tools provided by POD platforms:

- **POD Platforms Integrated Services:** Utilize the integrated services provided by POD platforms such as Printful, Printify, and Teelaunch to streamline order fulfillment and shipping processes. These platforms offer automated printing, packaging, and shipping services, allowing you to fulfill orders seamlessly without the need for manual intervention. Integrate your online store with your chosen POD platform to sync product listings, track inventory levels, and manage orders efficiently in real time. You can provide your customers with a transparent and reliable fulfillment experience by using advanced features like order tracking, batch processing, and shipping notifications.

- **Customer Support Tools and Automations:** Implement customer support tools and automations to enhance the quality and efficiency of your customer service operations. Use helpdesk software like Zendesk, Freshdesk, or Gorgias to manage customer inquiries, support tickets, and feedback across multiple channels, including email, live chat, and social media. Set up automated responses and workflows to handle common queries, escalate urgent issues, and prioritize high-value customers. You can also leverage chatbots to provide instant responses and personalized assistance, resulting in faster response times and improving customer satisfaction.

- **Quality Assurance and Returns Management:** Prioritize quality assurance measures to ensure the accuracy, consistency, and durability of your POD products. Regularly inspect printed merchandise, monitor production workflows, and collaborate closely with printing partners to maintain high product standards and minimize defects. Establish clear policies and procedures for handling returns, exchanges, and refunds, and communicate them transparently to customers to instill confidence in your brand and alleviate potential hesitations.

- **Customer Support Tools and Automations:** Implement customer support tools and automation to enhance the quality and efficiency of your customer service operations. Use helpdesk software like Zendesk, Freshdesk, or Gorgias to manage customer inquiries, support tickets, and feedback across multiple channels, including email, live chat, and social media. Set up automated responses and workflows to handle common queries, escalate urgent issues, and prioritize high-value customers. You can also use chatbots to provide instant responses and personalized assistance, reducing response times and improving customer satisfaction.

Step 7: Monitor & Optimize Shop Performance

To ensure the success and growth of your POD business, it's essential to monitor and optimize its performance continuously. Here's how you can leverage analytics tools and A/B testing to track key metrics, gain insights, and improve your business:

- **Analytics Tools:** Use analytics tools such as Google Analytics, Facebook Insights, and Instagram Insights to track and analyze various performance metrics across your online store and marketing channels. Monitor website traffic, conversion rates, average order value, and customer demographics to understand user behavior, identify trends, and measure the effectiveness of your marketing efforts. Leverage custom dashboards, reports, and data visualization tools to gain actionable insights and make informed decisions to optimize your business strategy. If you have someone running ads for you or managing your email campaign, they should be able to monitor these for you and interpret the data so that you can adjust your marketing efforts accordingly.

- **A/B Testing:** Compare different variations of your website, landing pages, product pages, and marketing campaigns to determine which performs better in terms of conversion and engagement. Test elements such as headlines, images, call-to-action buttons, pricing, and messaging to identify the most effective combinations that resonate with your target audience and drive desired outcomes. Use A/B testing tools provided by platforms like Google Optimize, Optimizely, or VWO to set up experiments, track results, and analyze statistical significance to make data-driven decisions.

As we've discovered, the POD business model is a great way for both seasoned and aspiring entrepreneurs to run a successful online business and market original ideas. If you're a creative entrepreneur or designer who has fun with marketing or selling visual goods, print-on-demand may be the perfect business model for you.

66

"The **internet** is becoming the **town square** for the global village of **tomorrow**."

– BILL GATES –

Chapter 9: Business Idea #5

Online Agency

One notable example of the Online Agency business model is Ladybugz, a digital marketing agency that began during the pandemic in the hopes of being able to work from home without compromising quality. Founder Lysa Miller was inspired to bring together digital experts of all kinds, including web designers and copywriters, to help business owners improve their online presence.

Launching over 40 websites in just its first year, Ladybugz now has 19 experts who each specialize in quite niche verticals, from biotech to non-profits. They also have quite a narrow target audience: Boston-based legacy brands.

This boutique agency is now continually named Boston's best and is only continuing to grow within their narrow niche. This is just one of the many ways online agencies can grow, expand their service offerings, and become known for their unique ways in which they provide value to clients. With that, let's explore the online agency business model and what makes it so special.

What Is an Online Agency?

An online agency, also known as a digital agency, is a business that provides a range of digital services to clients seeking to establish and enhance their online presence. These services typically include website design and development, search engine optimization, pay-per-click (PPC) advertising, social media management, content marketing, email marketing, and more. Online agencies leverage digital channels and platforms to help clients reach their target audience, drive traffic, generate leads, and achieve their business objectives online.

Unlike the service arbitrage business model we discussed in Chapter 6, where companies act as intermediaries, outsourcing tasks to third-party service providers, online agencies often have in-house experts who directly deliver services to clients. This allows for greater control over quality, consistency, and client relationships, enabling online agencies to provide more comprehensive and tailored solutions to meet their clients' needs in a more holistic way.

As consumers spend more time online and businesses recognize the value of digital channels for reaching and engaging their audience, the demand for online agency services continues to soar. In fact, global digital advertising spending is projected to surpass $600 billion in the next few years (Statista).

Let's look at the five most common types of online agencies:

- **Social Media Marketing Agencies:** Social media marketing agencies create and execute strategies to promote businesses on social media platforms. They focus on increasing brand awareness, engaging with the target audience, driving traffic, and generating leads or sales through platforms such as Facebook, Instagram, LinkedIn, and others. Services may include content creation, community management, paid advertising, influencer partnerships, and analytics tracking.

- **Design Agencies:** Design agencies specialize in visual communication and creative design. They work on projects ranging from graphic design, branding, and logo creation to web design, user interface design, and product packaging. Design agencies collaborate with clients to develop visually appealing and effective solutions that communicate their brand identity, values, and messaging to their target audience—you'll see many of these common themes and desired outcomes emerge throughout all types of the online agency business model.

- **Branding Agencies:** Branding agencies focus on developing and managing brands to create a distinct and memorable identity in the marketplace. They work closely with clients to define their brand strategy, positioning, messaging, and visual elements such as logos, color palettes, typography, and brand guidelines. Branding agencies help businesses establish a strong brand presence, build brand equity, and differentiate themselves from competitors through consistent branding across all touchpoints.

- **SEO Agencies:** Search Engine Optimization agencies specialize in organically improving a website's visibility and ranking on search engine results pages. They employ various techniques and strategies to optimize websites for search engines, such as keyword research, on-page optimization, technical SEO, content creation, link building, and performance tracking. SEO agencies help businesses increase their organic traffic, attract relevant leads, and enhance their online presence through higher search engine rankings.

- **Advertising Agencies:** Advertising agencies plan, create, and execute advertising campaigns across various media channels to promote products, services, or brands. They work with clients to develop advertising strategies, creative concepts, and messaging that resonate with the target audience. Advertising agencies handle print ads, digital ads, television commercials, radio spots, outdoor advertising, and more. They strive to engage the right audience effectively while achieving the client's marketing objectives and maximizing return on investment.

As businesses continue to allocate more resources to digital marketing and online advertising, the opportunities for online agencies to thrive and succeed are abundant. With the right strategies, expertise, and innovative approach, aspiring entrepreneurs can capitalize on the growing potential of the online agency industry to build successful and profitable businesses that provide a wide range of on-demand services.

Scoring the Online Agency Business

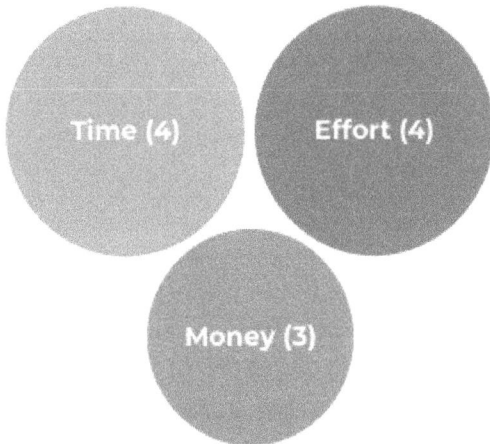

Time (4)

Effort (4)

Money (3)

Time: 4/5

An online agency requires a lot of time to get started. From the start of client acquisition to overseeing operations when you first hire people, this business model insists on a time investment.

Money: 3/5

The online agency business model requires moderate startup costs compared to traditional agencies and holds the potential for high profit margins. While the initial financial barrier to entry may be lower since it's all online, the more money you're able to invest from the start, the better. For instance, investing in a professional online presence and all that's needed to start hiring will require some capital.

Effort: 4/5

Running an online agency demands considerable dedication due to the potential involvement of multiple employees and the management of many projects simultaneously. Full-service agencies handle various custom projects with diverse service offerings, intensifying the workload even more and adding on employees as service offerings expand. The online agency space is also quite competitive, so continually adapting and maintaining a competitive edge is necessary, especially for those just starting out.

Start an Online Agency

- Step 1: Establishing Your Brand
- Step 2: Build Your Online Presence
- Step 3: Acquire Clients and Build Relationships
- Step 4: Streamline Day-to-Day Operations
- Step 5: Scale & Expand Your Offerings

Step 1: Establishing Your Brand

Before launching your online agency, it's essential to define your unique selling point (USP), determine your service offerings, assemble your team, and create an ideal client persona. Here's how to get started:

- **Define Your Unique Selling Point (USP):** Identify what sets your agency apart from the competition. Consider your strengths, expertise, and the value proposition you offer to clients. Whether it's specialized skills, innovative technology, or a unique approach to branding, your USP should resonate with your target audience and differentiate your agency in the marketplace.

- **Determine Your Service Offerings:** Determine the range of services you'll offer to clients based on your expertise, market demand, and competitive landscape. This may include web design, SEO, PPC advertising, social media management, content marketing, email marketing, analytics, and more. Tailor your service offerings to address the specific needs and pain points of your target market, ensuring alignment with your USP and value proposition identified earlier.

- **Hire the Right People:** Assemble a talented and diverse team of professionals to support your agency's operations and deliver exceptional service to clients. Depending on your service offerings and business model, this may include web developers, graphic designers, copywriters, SEO specialists, PPC experts, social media managers, project managers, and sales professionals. Look for individuals with relevant skills, experience, and cultural fit to contribute to your agency's success and give customers a reliable experience they keep coming back to. You can consider using job posting platforms like LinkedIn and Indeed, attending networking events and industry-specific meetups to connect with potential candidates, and leveraging online communities and forums for referrals. You can also explore freelancer platforms to outsource work on a project-by-project basis, but as you're getting started, hiring a part-time or permanent team is typically a more stable option. During the hiring process, evaluate candidates' compatibility with your agency's values and team dynamics, and administer skills assessments to gauge proficiency in relevant areas before choosing people. By carefully selecting those who possess the right skills, experience, and cultural compatibility, you can build a team that is passionate about delivering exceptional service and driving the success of your agency.

- **Create an Ideal Client Persona:** Develop detailed profiles of your ideal clients based on demographic, psychographic, and behavioral characteristics. Consider industry, company size, location, budget, pain points, goals, and buying behavior. Use market research, surveys, interviews, and data analysis to gain insights into your target audience and tailor your marketing strategies, messaging, and service offerings to meet their needs effectively. Create buyer personas using tools like HubSpot's Make My Persona or Xtensio's Persona Creator to visualize and understand your target audience's characteristics, preferences, and pain points. Once you identify this persona, you can cater your marketing efforts toward this ideal client.

Step 2: Build Your Online Presence

After defining your unique selling point and service offerings, assembling your team, and creating client personas, it's time to build the business and establish an online presence. Here's how to get started:

- **Craft Your Brand Identity:** Develop a compelling brand identity that reflects your agency's values, mission, and personality. This includes creating a memorable brand name, designing a professional logo, selecting brand colors and fonts, and crafting a unique brand voice and tone. Consistency is key across all brand touchpoints, from your website and social media profiles to your marketing materials and client communications.

- **Build a Professional Website:** Your website serves as the digital storefront for your agency and is often the first impression potential clients will have of your business. Invest in building a professional, user-friendly website that showcases your services, portfolio, team members, testimonials, and contact information. Ensure your website is mobile-responsive, optimized for search engines, and effectively reflects your brand identity and value proposition.

- **Create Compelling Content:** Content marketing is a powerful tool for building brand awareness, establishing thought leadership, and attracting and engaging your target audience. Develop a content strategy that aligns with your business goals and target audience's interests and preferences. Create high-quality blog posts, articles, case studies, videos, infographics, and other content assets that provide value, solve problems, and showcase your expertise in your niche.

- **Optimize for Search Engines:** Optimizing your website for search engines will Improve your agency's visibility and organic search rankings. Conduct keyword research to identify relevant keywords and phrases related to your services and target audience's needs. Optimize your website's on-page elements, including title tags, meta descriptions, headings, and content, to align with your target keywords and improve search engine visibility. Additionally, focus on building quality backlinks from reputable websites to boost your website's authority and credibility in the eyes of search engines.

- **Establish a Strong Social Media Presence:** Leverage social media platforms to engage with your audience, amplify your brand message, and drive traffic to your website. Choose the social media channels that align with your target audience's preferences and demographics, whether it's LinkedIn, Facebook, Instagram, or others.

Step 3: Acquire Clients and Build Relationships

Once you've defined and established your brand, it's time to start serving clients. Here's how to effectively acquire clients and foster meaningful connections that secure repeat business:

- **Develop a Sales Strategy:** Develop a comprehensive sales strategy to guide your client acquisition efforts and maximize conversion rates. This may include outbound prospecting, inbound marketing, networking events, cold outreach, referrals, partnerships, and strategic alliances. Highlight your past successes, case studies, testimonials, and client testimonials to demonstrate the tangible results you've achieved for previous clients.

- **Nurture Client Relationships:** Focus on building long-term relationships with clients by prioritizing communication, transparency, and responsiveness. Listen actively to their needs, concerns, and feedback, and proactively address any issues or challenges that arise. Keep clients informed about project progress, milestones, and results. Regularly check in to ensure they are satisfied and to identify any opportunities for upselling or cross-selling additional services.

Step 4: Streamline Day-to-Day Operations

Once you've acquired clients and secured projects, it's time to implement effective project management systems and streamline operations to ensure smooth execution and delivery. Here's how to effectively manage everyone involved and start streamlining your processes to help you scale:

- **Choose the Right Project Management Tools:** Select a robust project management tool or software that aligns with your agency's workflow. Whether it's

Asana, Trello, Monday.com, or Basecamp, ensure the chosen platform offers features such as task assignment, deadlines, progress tracking, file sharing, and communication capabilities to facilitate collaboration and transparency among team members. It's best to choose an all-in-one platform instead of using different communication platforms that may have your team scattered and disorganized.

- **Define Clear Processes and Workflows:** Establish clear processes and workflows for each stage of the project lifecycle, from initial client onboarding and project kick-off to execution, delivery, and post-project evaluation. Document standard operating procedures (SOPs), project templates, and checklists to ensure consistency, efficiency, and quality across all projects. Communicate expectations, roles, and responsibilities to team members to minimize confusion and maximize productivity.

Step 5: Scale & Expand Your Offerings

As your online agency grows, it's essential to focus on scaling your business and expanding your service offerings. Here are a few ways to start growing your business once it's established:

- **Assess Your Growth Trajectory:** Evaluate your agency's current performance, financial health, and growth trajectory to determine if it's the right time to scale. Consider revenue growth, client retention rates, market demand, and your competitors. Assess your agency's strengths, weaknesses, opportunities, and threats (SWOT analysis) to identify areas for improvement and potential growth avenues.

- **Invest in Infrastructure:** Invest in the necessary infrastructure, resources, and technology to support your agency's expansion. This may include upgrading your project management systems, investing in automation tools, hiring additional staff, and expanding your office space or remote work capabilities.

- **Expand Your Service Offerings:** Diversify your service offerings to cater to a broader range of client needs and preferences. Consider adding new services such as marketing automation, conversion rate optimization, video production, podcasting, or emerging technologies like machine learning that are in high demand. Conduct market research and client surveys to identify new opportunities and validate demand for these new services before investing resources in their development and launch.

- **Develop Strategic Partnerships:** Form alliances with complementary businesses, agencies, vendors, and industry experts to augment your capabilities and reach new markets. Collaborate with partners to offer integrated solutions, cross-promotional opportunities, and joint ventures that add value to your clients and differentiate your agency in the marketplace. For instance, if your agency offers branding but you want to venture into web development, you could connect with web developers, designers, and other professionals offering these services.

- **Focus on Client Retention:** Prioritize client satisfaction as you scale your business, as existing clients are often your most valuable asset. Invest in building strong relationships, delivering exceptional service, and exceeding client expectations to ensure repeat business. Implement feedback mechanisms, conduct client surveys, and regularly communicate with clients to gather insights, address concerns, and identify opportunities for improvement.

- **Continue Hiring and Building Teams:** In this phase of scaling, hiring becomes pivotal, even if you already have a team. Identify key roles that need to be filled to support your growth objectives and focus on hiring talented individuals who align with your agency's culture, values, and vision. This doesn't mean full time salaried staff but leveraging freelancers and VA's to support your growth.

When running an online agency, one theme remains constant: the importance of understanding your audience and connecting with the right clients. By identifying your niche and catering to these clients, you establish a place for your agency in the market and lay the groundwork for sustainable growth.

However, the online agency business model is best for entrepreneurs looking to be more hands-on in their business. Running an online agency requires more time and investment compared to models like dropshipping or print-on-demand. It involves managing a wide range of services, clients, and team members. However, this makes it an extra lucrative opportunity for those who want to have a larger business with a wide range of service offerings one day.

Part Three: Your Future Business

66

"**Success** demands **singleness** of purpose."

– VINCE LOMBARDI –

Chapter 10: Laser Focus

The most successful entrepreneurs of our time share one thing in common: *specialization*. Of course, many serial entrepreneurs own and invest in multiple businesses, but most CEOs and world-famous celebrities are known for doing *one* thing really well.

One example to understand this idea can be found in the athlete Michael Phelps, the most decorated Olympian of all time. Phelps gained momentum by participating in various swimming events, displaying his versatility across different strokes and distances. However, it wasn't until he focused his efforts on specific events and strokes that he truly began to dominate the sport. Just like an entrepreneur who must carve out a niche in a large sector, Phelps began to make his own name in swimming.

He and his coach, Bob Bowman, identified the events where Phelps had the greatest potential for success, namely the individual medley and butterfly events. They homed in on these events, and Phelps dedicated himself to training specifically for these races, refining his technique, building his strength, and perfecting his racing strategy toward these more specific goals.

By specializing in these events, Phelps maximized his performance, narrowed his focus, and achieved unprecedented success in the pool. At the 2004 Olympic Games in Athens, he won six gold and two bronze medals, setting multiple world records. His success continued at the 2008 Beijing Olympics, where he won an astounding eight gold medals, surpassing Mark Spitz's record for the most gold medals won at a single Olympics.

By focusing on achieving new records within specific disciplines, Phelps could spend all his time focusing on specific goals, allowing him to surpass numerous records. Today, he has 28 Olympic medals and is known as one of the greatest athletes of all time.

With so many exciting opportunities out there, it can be hard to narrow our focus as entrepreneurs. Even knowing where to begin is anything but simple. In this chapter, we'll explore ways to identify your next best step in building a successful business and how to avoid being overwhelmed in the process. Just as Phelps made a name for himself in particular swimming events, you can also make a name for yourself in the industry you love. To start, we must get specific about choosing your initial business path.

Choosing Your Business Path

"One of the huge mistakes people make is that they try to force an interest on themselves. You don't choose your passions; your passions choose you."

– Jeff Bezos –

Of course, after making your way through this book, it may seem that there are countless directions ahead of you. Rest assured that there is no right or wrong choice. There is no best business idea that will be the key to your success. The best business idea is the one you are willing to start and work hard at to make it succeed. The key lies in discovering what aligns with your strengths and passions. To guide your choice, ask yourself the following questions:

- What are you passionate about? What keeps you motivated even when challenges arise? Choosing a business idea that aligns with your passions can keep you interested and motivated in the long run.

- What skills do you already have? How can you leverage these strengths to bring your idea to fruition? Building upon what you excel at can enhance your chances of success and flatten your learning curve.

- What opportunities and gaps do you currently see in the market? Is there a need or desire for the product or service you're considering? Understanding market demand can inform your decision and help you focus on ideas with the potential for viability and growth.

- How big of an impact can your business idea have on the world or the community you hope to help? Consider the potential impact of each idea, not only in terms of financial returns but also its contribution to society, the environment, or other meaningful causes.

By evaluating these criteria and listening to your intuition, you can choose a path that feels authentic and rewarding to you. Remember to use the VANS criteria we outlined in Chapter 4 to validate your chosen business idea; it must always fit the criteria of being a business system.

The Power of a Singular Focus

"People think focus means saying yes to the thing you've got to focus on. But that's not what it means at all."
– Steve Jobs –

In the words of Steve Jobs, "People think focus means saying yes to the thing you've got to focus on. But that's not what it means at all." True focus isn't about juggling multiple endeavors; it's about the deliberate act of saying no to distractions and honing in on what truly matters to you. It's about embracing specialization over generalization, much like how Michael Phelps didn't conquer all swimming events but channeled his efforts into specific ones.

To excel as a business leader, you must cultivate specialized expertise rather than attempting to be a jack of all trades. In other words, you must become the *master of one*. One study shows that focusing on a single business niche increases the likelihood of success by 33% compared to those who diversify their efforts across multiple areas (Harvard Business School). By concentrating on a particular area, you not only enhance your skills rapidly but also carve out a distinct niche in the market. This singularity of focus not only streamlines your efforts but also makes it easier to allocate resources and recruit the right talent for your team.

Embracing a singular focus entails committing to one business model, one niche, one product, and one audience. This means going deep rather than spreading yourself thin. You must fully immerse yourself in a single domain, positioning yourself as an expert and authority whose knowledge and insights command attention and respect.

You have a limited amount of time and attention, and spreading this across several ventures will mean you won't succeed in any of them.

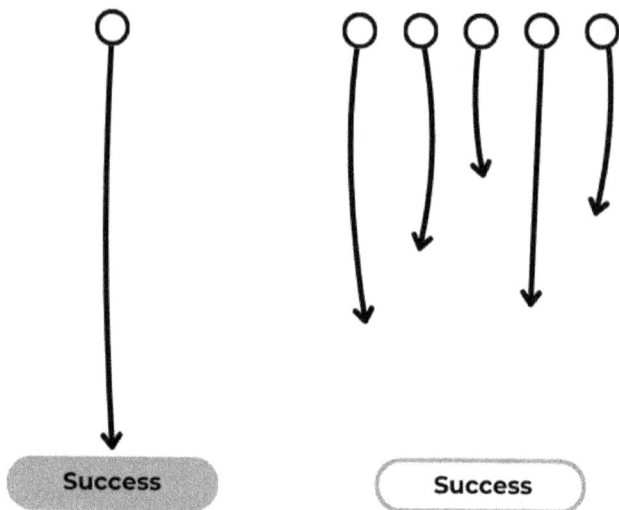

Fig 4: Illustrates how spreading our energy across multiple ventures restricts our ability to achieve success.

Remember, there should be no room for a plan B. Contingency plans only dilute your commitment to your primary goal. While it may be tempting for entrepreneurs to constantly pursue new opportunities, the most successful businesspeople of our time are those who remain dedicated to a specific goal and don't stop until they have accomplished exactly what their initial vision was. As the saying goes, "A ship with two captains sinks." Dividing your attention between multiple ideas only serves to weaken your resolve and diminish your chances of success.

Ironically, when you spend time becoming an expert in one area, you minimize your room for mistakes in the long run. Going deep into a single area allows you to become the go-to expert on that topic (more on this in Chapter 12) and command an audience automatically. Your value proposition will be so specific that they will have no choice but to choose you for that product or service.

Multiple Income Streams – What It Means for You

All aspiring entrepreneurs hear the same sentiment: the average millionaire has seven streams of income. The concept of multiple income streams is a hot topic that promises financial security and abundance. In my last book, *9 Money Habits Keeping You Poor*, we discussed the importance of building multiple streams of income. However, it's important to note that pursuing multiple income streams follows attaining initial success in one endeavor. Ultimately, from the business ideas we have shared in this book, you can and should aspire to do all of them one day; however, it's critical that you start with *one*.

We can see this in lots of success stories, as virtually every successful entrepreneur can trace their journey back to a single breakthrough—a pivotal moment when their passion, talent, and hard work converged to propel them to new heights.

For instance, Elon Musk's early wins with PayPal paved the way for his ventures into space with SpaceX and Tesla.

Similarly, Oprah Winfrey's ascent from local news anchor to media mogul began with her talk show, which then kick-started her major media empire.

The key distinction here is that the pursuit of multiple income streams is not a strategy unto itself but rather a natural progression that arises from initial success. It is the fruit of labor diligently sown in a singular field of expertise—*specialization precedes diversification*.

However, you may see this as a contradiction. After all, isn't the idea of multiple income streams about spreading one's efforts across various ventures from the outset? While this does happen in certain contexts, it overlooks the foundational principle that often underpins sustainable success: *mastery*.

Most of the time, multiple income streams aren't a shortcut to success. They provide a way for entrepreneurs to naturally progress and master their craft. By focusing on excelling in a single domain, we lay the groundwork for future diversification, ensuring that each new stream of income flows from a foundation of proven expertise and experience. This makes success much more sustainable in the end.

The 25% Rule for Entrepreneurs

If you're new to entrepreneurship, it may be tempting to think of a single, large end goal in mind and use that goal to motivate you. However, it's more productive to break this large end goal into smaller goals that will keep you motivated along the way. This is especially important if you're new to starting a business.

The 25% Rule advocates for the systematic breakdown of any target or goal into smaller, more attainable increments. By dividing the journey into halves (100%>50%) and then halves again (50%>25%), we transform major goals into small, manageable objectives that are both actionable and achievable. Taking an incremental approach not only reduces being overwhelmed but also provides tangible markers of progress to keep us motivated along the way.

Picture climbing a mountain. As you begin your ascent, the summit looms large in the distance, seemingly out of reach. Days pass, yet the peak appears no closer than when you first set out. It's easy to feel disheartened and question whether the summit will ever be within grasp.

However, by applying the 25% Rule, you refract this huge journey into digestible segments. By halving the distance, then halving again, reaching the 25% point in the journey becomes your first milestone that fuels your determination and makes you feel more accomplished in reaching the end goal.

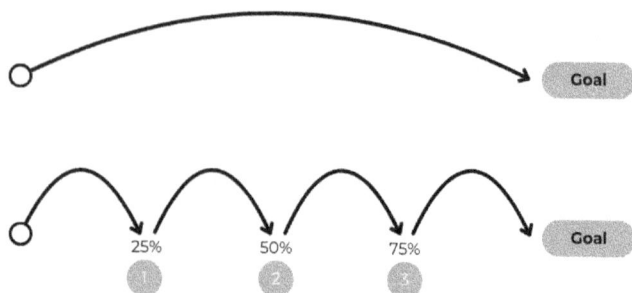

Fig 5: Shows the breakdown of a large goal into smaller attainable targets using the 25% rule.

It's not uncommon for aspiring entrepreneurs to have large goals. In the context of these goals, this rule can give us clarity and purpose. Whether you're launching a new business or expanding into new markets, the core principle remains the same: break it down, conquer it step by step, and celebrate each milestone along the way.

Setting Milestones

"Setting goals is the first step in turning the invisible into the visible."

– Tony Robbins –

Using the 25% rule, setting milestones will allow you to start small and scale steadily. Rather than focusing on lofty income targets or overnight success, we strive for more incremental growth by setting realistic and achievable milestones. When it comes to generating income, we should begin with a simple target of $1,000 per month and then build from there.

Why start with 1k a month, you may ask? Firstly, we need to see if our business idea is viable by aiming for a monthly turnover of 1k per month. If we can't generate this modest sum, it forces us to reassess our strategy and pivot if necessary. Conversely, reaching this milestone validates the potential of our concept, signaling that we're onto something worth pursuing.

Moreover, hitting the 1k mark isn't just about revenue. It signifies that we've taken an idea from conception to execution, transforming it into a tangible source of income. This not only validates us as entrepreneurs but also solidifies the necessary entrepreneurial qualities we went over in Part 1—having an Entrepreneurial Mindset.

But the journey doesn't end at 1k per month; it's only the first step on our path. Once we've proven the viability of our business model, the next step is to scale our efforts. Here is where exponential growth comes into play. By doubling our efforts—repeating the process to reach 2k, then 4k, and so on—we unlock the potential for true expansion.

The pursuit of early wins is not a one-and-done strategy—it's a mindset. It involves striving for excellence and always aiming to outdo the competition. As Phil Knight, founder of Nike, once said, "Play by the rules but be ferocious." The entrepreneurial spirit involves a delicate balance between integrity and tenacity, between fair play and unwavering determination.

To maintain a strong work ethic over the years, you must embrace the grind—push past your limits each day and pursue your end goal without losing sight of it. But excellence alone is not enough; you must also be better than the competition. In a world where success is measured not by participation but by domination, the stakes are high. Running a successful business requires more than skill or talent—it demands a "going to war" mindset—a willingness to do whatever it takes to win.

Key Takeaways

- Choose a business idea that works for you. There is no right or wrong choice.

- Success demands singleness of purpose and laser-like focus in achieving goals.

- Specialization drives success. Successful entrepreneurs excel in one area before branching out.

- Use early successes as stepping stones to future triumphs. Each victory builds momentum and confidence for what lies ahead.

- Set a small target to measure the viability of your business idea.

- Strategy, innovation, and determination are key to overcoming competition. Play by the rules but be relentless in your pursuit of success.

66

"The **will** to win, the **desire** to succeed, the **urge** to reach your full potential. These are the keys that will **unlock** the door to personal **excellence**."

– CONFUCIUS –

Chapter 11: Winners Are Made – Not Born

When I decided to leave my job as a car salesman and start my journey in the business world, it was an incredibly exciting time. I had a clear objective, a detailed plan, and all the motivation I thought I needed. I was eager to go!

Throughout my life, I have always followed a set of procedures or step-by-step instructions to achieve desired outcomes. If I was scientific in my approach, the results would naturally follow. So, as a new entrepreneur ready to start my food and beverage business, I meticulously planned every single step. I found a great location, came up with the perfect brand name, and created a great menu. What could go wrong? Reality hit hard when my first venture crumbled beneath me. It didn't just fail; it failed spectacularly!

Initially, it showed promise. We were busy, sales were strong, and we all rode the wave of excitement that comes with a new business. However, it all started heading south soon after. I didn't have a marketing plan, so maintaining relevance and building a following suffered. I thought I just had to offer great food, but if your customers don't know about it, how will they find you? Managing staff and keeping them happy took way too much of my time, so I couldn't focus on day-to-day admin of the business. Who would have thought that paper towel prices would be so high or that you must order bottled water from a different supplier than ketchup bottles?

It was a bitter pill to swallow because I did not know at the time that this failure, and failure in general, would be the greatest teacher in my entrepreneurship journey. I thought as an entrepreneur in the food business, I needed to know about food. I only realized afterward that there is knowing about food as a layperson and knowing food as a business expert. The difference is vast. Furthermore, being an entrepreneur in the food business doesn't stop there—you need to have equal expertise in sales, marketing, accounting, and therapy!

Although my first business failed, it provided the best education in business I could have ever asked for—better than any course or degree could offer. Looking back, it wasn't a failure but rather the foundation for all my future successes.

We live in a world that often punishes us for failure. Entrepreneurs who take risks, as they should, are often perceived as those who live on the edge and should be afraid to fail in the name of playing it safe. Corporate jobs often reward playing it safe and discourage innovation and cross-functional collaboration with colleagues. But in a society that often stigmatizes failure, we must reframe our mindset to view it as a valuable opportunity for *growth*.

Like a musician honing their craft, mastery in business takes time and dedication. It's about acquiring the necessary skills, whether it's in entrepreneurship, management, or the intricacies of our specific industry. And just as every note played contributes to the creation of a wonderful song, every skill acquired brings us closer to our entrepreneurial vision, which is why we've gone through so many of these skills throughout this book.

Failure is an *inevitable* part of starting a business, but it doesn't mean that success is impossible. In fact, failure and success often go hand in hand. Those who experience failure most often are the ones who give themselves the most opportunities to succeed.

Failure is Essential for Success

"The most valuable thing you can make is a mistake - you can't learn anything from being perfect."

– Adam Osborne –

To truly understand why we need failure, we must first adopt a long-term perspective. Success should be measured by our ability to bounce back and learn from our setbacks, not just immediate wins. The myth of natural talent diminishes the significance of hard work, perseverance, and the willingness to learn from failure—all skills we can build as entrepreneurs, and these do not have to be innate traits. By shifting the focus from short-term gains to long-term growth, we set the stage for a mindset conducive to embracing failure as a stepping stone to success.

In the ever-evolving world of entrepreneurship and building a business, the adage "fail fast, learn faster" rings true. Rapid experimentation and iteration allow us to quickly identify what works and what doesn't, allowing for timely strategic pivots and adaptations. Rather than fearing failure, we should embrace it as a catalyst for innovation and progress—it's the feedback that tells us what we're doing wrong and what we need to change.

With that being said, there is indeed a right way to fail as an entrepreneur, and it's failing *fast* and *cheap*. It's about strategically navigating setbacks with efficiency and resourcefulness. Instead of taking complete risks, strive for small, manageable goals. That way, if you do fail, it will lead to small, manageable failures that yield valuable insights. Failure is inevitable but not insurmountable in the process of building a business. That's why we must prioritize rapid experimentation and iteration, valuing each lesson we learn without incurring unnecessary expenses or delays. The goal is not to avoid failure altogether but to fail *intelligently*. This means extracting maximum value from each setback while maintaining momentum toward our goals. So, we must embrace and seek failure, but we want to do it as quickly and inexpensively as possible.

Failure provides a unique learning opportunity that cannot be replicated through success alone. We must try something first to see if it works and how we can improve. Yet, our education system and traditional jobs often punish failure, ingraining in us a fear of making mistakes. As entrepreneurs, we must unlearn this fear and reframe failure as a valuable teacher on our journey to success.

Through continual refinement of our ideas, processes, and strategies, we inch closer to our entrepreneurial goals. Each iteration builds upon the lessons learned from past failures, guiding us toward greater resilience and eventual success. This may involve fine-tuning a business until it meets market demand or tweaking an idea until it becomes viable.

The Dunning-Kruger Effect

"Many of life's failures are people who did not realize how close they were to success when they gave up."
– Thomas A. Edison –

We also have a tendency, not just as entrepreneurs but as humans, to overestimate our competence in a particular area, especially in the early stages of learning. This is known as the *Dunning-Kruger Effect*, a psychological phenomenon named after researchers David Dunning and Justin Kruger. It sheds light on a common cognitive bias that affects entrepreneurs and individuals across various domains. The effect refers to the tendency of people to believe they are smarter and more capable than they actually are. Essentially, individuals with low ability lack the skills to recognize their own incompetence. The combination of poor self-awareness and low cognitive ability leads them to overestimate their capabilities.

We have all experienced this at some point in our lives. For example, when you see a professional athlete on TV and think you can do it too. Only when you try to swing at the ball and completely miss, do you begin to realize it's a lot harder than it looks.

Understanding this idea is crucial, as you will go through this process in your journey as an entrepreneur. Recognizing your position in the process can be the difference between achieving success or giving up too early.

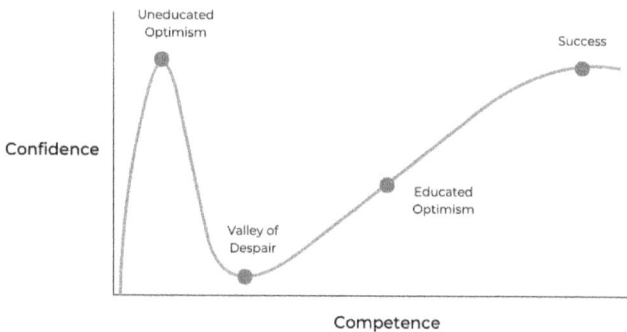

Fig 6: Charts the level of competence against confidence and shows key moments in the process.

If you look at the timeline of building competence in any discipline, it begins with the upward curve of being extremely confident and vastly overestimating your capabilities. We refer to this as uneducated optimism (like when I started my first business venture). As reality sets in and we realize it's harder than we thought, we slide down into the phase of educated pessimism. This bottoms out at our lowest confidence level and the valley of despair. This is a major crossroads; most people give up on an idea at this point and move on to try something new. This is a huge mistake. This humbling moment is when we need to double down and persevere to learn and build the skills needed to achieve success. Once we make the choice, that is when the magic happens. We start to gain educated optimism and our confidence gradually grows as we gain competence and head toward achievement and success.

Mastering Skills as Entrepreneurs

"Most people have no idea of the giant capacity we can immediately command when we focus all of our resources on mastering a single area of our lives."
– Tony Robbins –

Building on the Dunning-Kruger Effect, the road to achievement is built on developing *skills*. Once we have the realization of our limited knowledge in any discipline and fully commit to building skills, we can start gaining real competence and creating value that we can offer to the world. Like learning an instrument requires patience, practice, and persistence, mastery in entrepreneurship takes time. We must resist the temptation to rush our journey to success and instead embrace the process of gradual improvement, as mentioned in the last chapter, with the importance of setting and celebrating small milestones.

While a good idea and hard work are foundational, true success hinges upon our ability to develop and refine the necessary skills to navigate the complexities of business. It's not merely about having a vision but also about possessing the skills to execute it effectively.

Entrepreneurs often quickly realize the depth of their ignorance once they delve into the entrepreneurial journey, hence the Dunning-Kruger effect. However, it's those who diligently develop their skills that remain known in their field.

These skills extend beyond business acumen and encompass a deep understanding of the intricacies within one's industry. For instance, in e-commerce ventures, mastering search engine optimization or digital marketing can significantly impact success just as much as the process of setting up the business itself. Similarly, proficiency in both coding languages and project management techniques is indispensable in software development.

Persistence and Consistency: The Winning Formula

"If you really look closely, most overnight successes took a
long time."

– Steve Jobs –

Persistence and consistency emerge as the winning formula. Grit becomes a must-have as we weather the storms of entrepreneurship. How well we truly persevere can be seen in our daily habits.

By cultivating habits that foster productivity, creativity, and resilience, we lay the groundwork for sustainable growth and long-term success. Whether it's dedicating time each day to learning more about your industry, cultivating a growth mindset, or honing in on a particular skill, our daily habits shape our trajectory as entrepreneurs.

Every entrepreneur follows a unique timeline on their path to success as well. Think about all the case studies we've examined throughout this book and how each success story differs from one another. We can see that the differences remain constant no matter which successful business we take inspiration from.

Richard Branson is another great example of rapid iteration and diverse business ventures. As the founder of the Virgin Group, Richard is known for his willingness to take risks. He has experienced a series of successes and failures across diverse industries. Branson's approach embodies the idea of failing fast and learning faster. For example, Virgin Records, his first major success, came after numerous failed ventures in publishing and retail. His ability to pivot and adapt allowed him to build a conglomerate spanning music, airlines, telecommunications, and more, utilizing all his existing skill sets at once.

On the other hand, we can see perseverance and singular focus take place in Colonel Harland Sanders' journey. The founder of KFC epitomizes the value of sticking to one thing until getting it right. Sanders faced numerous rejections and setbacks throughout his life. It wasn't until he was in his sixties that he found success with his fried chicken recipe. Despite facing financial difficulties and over 1,000 rejections, Sanders persisted, eventually franchising KFC, and building it into a global fast-food empire.

Resilience, adaptability, and continuous learning are crucial in the face of failure and lessons. Whether we achieve success quickly or after years of perseverance, one thing will remain constant: we can always use failure as a catalyst for growth and innovation.

Key Takeaways

- Failure is essential for success because setbacks are opportunities for growth.

- Fail as quickly and cheaply as possible to gain the experiences needed to achieve success.

- Any new venture will follow the Dunning-Kruger Effect. Understand your position in the journey and recognize the launch point to achievement.

- Develop your skills to build you and your business.

- Every entrepreneur has their own unique timeline, but success is achieved through perseverance.

- Persistence and consistency are the winning formula, which is made up of our daily habits.

66

"Try not to become a man of **success**.
Rather become a man of **value**."

– ALBERT EINSTEIN –

Chapter 12: Create Exceptional Value

One company with a fascinating origin story that exemplifies creating exceptional value for customers is Adidas. It all began with a rift between two brothers, Adolf and Rudolf Dassler. In the early 1920s, the Dassler brothers started a small shoemaking business in their mother's laundry room in Herzogenaurach, Germany.

Unlike other business owners whose primary goal is making money, they were set on providing exceptional solutions to their ideal customers: athletes. They knew those customers had a problem they could solve through their innovative yet simple shoe designs, focusing on providing athletes with footwear that enhanced their performance.

During the 1936 Summer Olympics in Berlin, the brothers gained attention when American sprinter Jesse Owens (a perfect example of their ideal customer) wore their spikes and won four gold medals, bringing international recognition to the brand. Consequently, many other athletes were also drawn to the brand.

However, as their business grew, personal and professional conflicts between Adolf and Rudolf escalated. This tension eventually led to a permanent split in 1948, with Rudolf forming his own company, Puma, and Adolf renaming his portion of the business Adidas, derived from his nickname "Adi" and the first three letters of his last name.

Despite all of this, Adolf Dassler remained dedicated to his vision of creating high-quality athletic footwear that prioritized performance and comfort. It wasn't about fame or money for him. Instead, he was passionate about understanding the needs of athletes and incorporating their feedback into the design process. This customer-centric approach sets Adidas apart in the competitive sportswear market. They put their customers' needs at the forefront, and by solving them, they inevitably became a household name.

Adolf understood that by prioritizing the needs of athletes and delivering superior products, he could build a brand with a loyal following. This philosophy continues to drive Adidas's success today, with a focus on innovation, sustainability, and community engagement with athletes he knew he wanted to help from the get-go.

By staying true to their core principles and prioritizing the needs of their customers first, Adidas and other entrepreneurs can make a positive impact and provide value all around the world. Instead of starting with the sole goal of making a profit, entrepreneurs who begin with an objective to solve an ideal client or customer's problem will connect with them on a deeper level and, in turn, find long-term success.

Rethinking Your Entrepreneurial Objectives

"The world's biggest problems are also the world's biggest business opportunities. You want to become a billionaire? Help a billion people."

– Peter Diamandis –

In the pursuit of entrepreneurship, it's easy to get caught up in money as the main objective. However, the most successful entrepreneurs understand that true fulfillment lies not in the accumulation of wealth, but in the creation of value for others, which results in wealth creation, as we saw with Adidas.

When it comes to value creation, the larger the problem you solve and the more individuals you impact, the greater the value you create. For example, building a cutting-edge yacht that transforms the industry may solve a big problem, but it only impacts a small group of people. This will no doubt create wealth for the business, but not at the same level as a company like Google. Google founders Larry Page and Sergey Brin solved a big problem for millions of people by revolutionizing the online search engine, creating enormous value as a result. Alternatively, a banana slicer, which makes the task of cutting up a banana more convenient, is not a significant problem for most people, so it doesn't create much value at all.

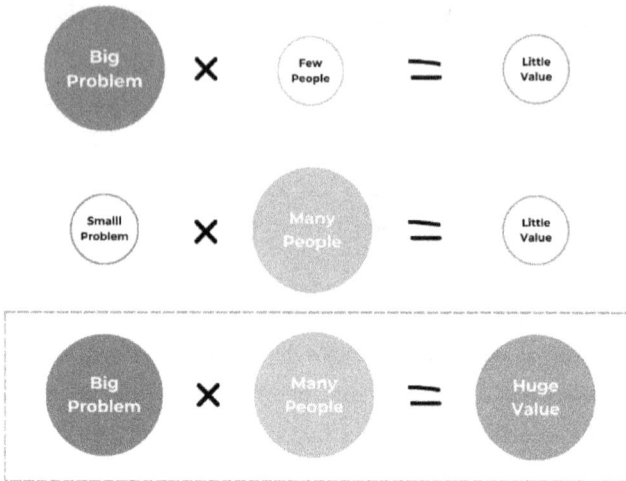

Fig 7: Demonstrates the formula of value creation based on the size of the problem and the number of people benefiting from the solution.

You might be wondering: is making money not important then? Absolutely not. Generating wealth is a fundamental objective of being an entrepreneur; however, it is not the primary goal. It is this crucial nuance that distinguishes successful entrepreneurs from those who fail in the long run.

As we approach the stages of putting all we've learned about building a business into action, you can start to think of making money as a capitalistic report card. It's a tangible measure of how much value you are providing to others. This perspective reframes financial success as a reflection of the impact you've had on people's lives rather than just a means to acquire more money or material items, and this mindset is often what keeps entrepreneurs motivated.

Entrepreneurs should strive for a deeper type of fulfillment. This comes from knowing that their work has made a meaningful difference in the world. Becoming rich isn't the ultimate goal; rather, it's a result of being a valuable contributor to society. When we see money as a byproduct of creating value, our focus shifts from personal enrichment to becoming a source of value for others. In fact, The Global Entrepreneurship Monitor found that entrepreneurs driven by a sense of purpose and passion for their work are three times more likely to achieve high growth compared to those who are solely motivated by financial gain. So, keep that in mind as we continue to brainstorm and apply ways to build your own business from a simple idea.

Finding the "Why" Behind Your Business

"There's lots of bad reasons to start a company. But there's only one good, legitimate reason, and I think you know what it is: it's to change the world."
– Phil Libin –

In the process of building a business, identifying your "why" is crucial. It's the driving force behind your business that will keep it alive for the years to come. Your passion for your product or service shapes it and becomes an integral part of its value proposition to the market.

In my previous book, *9 Money Habits Keeping You Poor*, I went into detail around the idea of generating new income streams and discussed the idea of an exchange of value. This is when someone gives you money in return for something valuable you provide. Your value offer is referred to as your value proposition.

A business's value proposition is an easy-to-understand reason why a customer should buy a product or service from that particular business. For example, Nike's brand value proposition is, "To provide fashionable, innovative, and high-performance shoes for customers in every sport to meet their changing demands."

As you shift from a consumer's mindset to a producer (as we covered in Chapter 2), you will need to understand what value proposition you want to offer to the world. This central idea will be the nucleus of who you are as an entrepreneur and will manifest in all activities related to your business.

There is a saying, "Painting behind the radiators." This refers to painting the parts of a room that no one can see, but people still do it because they are passionate about doing their best. Steve Jobs, the visionary co-founder of Apple, believed in this concept. As a young boy, he had helped his father build a fence around their backyard. His father emphasized the importance of using just as much care on the back of the fence as on the front. "Nobody will ever know," Steve said. His father replied, "But you will know." In overseeing the Apple II and the Macintosh, Jobs applied this lesson to the circuit board inside the machine. In both instances, he sent the engineers back to make the chips line up neatly so the board would look nice. "Nobody is going to see the PC board," one of them protested. Jobs reacted as his father had and replied, "I want it to be as beautiful as possible, even if it's inside the box."

This level of passion and perfection was weaved through all of Apple's products. It's no surprise that they are revered to such high standards and have an infamous reputation for quality. When you genuinely care about what you're offering to the world, it shines through in every aspect of your business. People can sense the authenticity and dedication you bring to your craft. In contrast, if your sole focus is on chasing money, it becomes evident in the quality of your product or service. Customers are quick to recognize when a business lacks passion and is driven solely by profit motives.

The customer experience is greatly influenced by the care and attention you put into your business. When you prioritize delivering value and solving problems for your customers, it fosters trust and loyalty. Conversely, if your primary goal is to maximize profits at the expense of customer satisfaction, it's likely to be rejected by the market in the long run.

At the heart of every successful brand is an emotional connection with its customers. One survey conducted by Salesforce found that 79% of customers are more likely to buy from a company that demonstrates they understand and care about their needs. But people don't just buy products or services; they buy into the story, the ethos, and the emotional essence of a brand. What emotions does your product or service evoke in your customers? Understanding and leveraging this emotional connection is key to building a strong brand and effective marketing strategy that converts. If you also have an emotional connection to your brand, you'll love going to work every day despite the hardships of building a business.

Your "why" forms the foundation of your brand identity and influences every aspect of your business, from product development to marketing messaging. By aligning your passion with the needs and desires of your target audience, you can create a powerful value proposition that resonates deeply and gets people to buy.

Being a Value-Centric Entrepreneur

"A business is simply an idea to make other people's lives better."

– Richard Branson –

Understanding value creation is at the core of being a successful entrepreneur. On top of generating revenue, you are building bridges that connect you to your customers and improve their lives. Instead of chasing mirages of quick profits, focus on creating lasting, meaningful value.

To achieve this, you need to understand that it is about your customer, not you. In Chapter 10, we discussed the importance of having a single focus, which included understanding who your customer is. They need to be vivid and tangible in your mind, so you can truly get into their shoes and understand what you can offer them. Your customers don't care about your sales targets or personal goals in life—all they care about is what is in it for them. The value proposition you offer them must be exceptional and aim to blow them away.

Example Area	Basic Value	Exceptional Value
Delivery and service	Online ordering with a reasonable delivery time of 3-5 working days and 30 days return policy with postage not included.	Amazon Prime offers next-day delivery with an extended returns policy, including a pickup service, often with no charge to the customer.
Variety and simplicity	Ordering or renting single movies and box sets by mail or at a store for a fixed fee.	Netflix provides a simple subscription service with a vast catalog and simplicity in streaming media from anywhere.

Example Area	Basic Value	Exceptional Value
Sustainability and environment	Offering quality apparel to the market at a competitive price and focusing on offshore production.	Patagonia prioritizes sustainability and social responsibility in their production, using recycled materials, promoting fair labor practices, and donating a percentage of their profits to environmental causes.

These examples highlight the difference between ordinary and extraordinary. You should strive to deliver the latter.

Furthermore, what is your Unique Selling Point (USP)? Your USP needs to go beyond being adequate and instead stand out as remarkable. Let's take another look at Adidas. The founders didn't just offer a USP for their products that was merely decent; they developed revolutionary lightweight and comfortable sports shoes that other competitors could not manufacture.

This is why at the heart of every business is recognizing the importance of care and purpose. True success comes from enriching the lives of others and contributing positively to society. This requires redefining wealth into a more holistic definition that encompasses financial prosperity, personal fulfillment, and societal impact on a broader scale.

Defining your purpose as an entrepreneur is essential. Ask yourself:

- Who do I want to serve?

- What problems do I want to solve?

- How can I make a meaningful difference in the lives of my ideal customers?

- How can I solve their problems better than anyone else out there?

Aligning your business with your values and passions creates a powerful sense of purpose that drives you forward. It's important to understand that value creation is a nonlinear process. Building value requires consistent effort and dedication to consistently deliver excellence to your customers. However, once you've established a strong value proposition, you'll experience exponential returns that surpass your initial efforts.

Remember, value creation is greater than wealth accumulation. While wealth may be a byproduct of creating value, it should not be the sole focus of building your business. Your business should prioritize creating value first, knowing that wealth will naturally follow.

This mindset shift may not be easy at first. I remember when I first began my car detailing business after failing in the food & beverage space. I knew I had to look at things differently the second time around to find lasting success. So, I reflected on the skills and knowledge I already had to see how I could bring value to the market. I asked myself those same questions above, brainstorming about who I could serve and how I could solve their problems better than anyone else.

Since I already had experience with cars and understood my ideal client, I was confident that I could offer a more holistic local detailing service than anyone else out there. I was set on solving my ideal clients' needs, and this perspective changed my life. Instead of solely focusing on money, I was focusing on serving a target audience I was familiar with. My goal was to provide more value than anyone else by offering the most comprehensive car detailing service out there, from leather trimming to glass cleaning. I knew they would have no other choice but to choose me as their go-to spot for getting their car detailed.

By establishing ourselves as the top destination for value, we began seeing a significant increase in revenue, and I could use my skills to solve their problems better than our competitors.

Key Takeaways

- Reorient your entrepreneurial objectives from solely focusing on profit to prioritizing the creation of value for your customers and society.

- Discover your passion and purpose as an entrepreneur. Align your business with your values and aspirations to create a deeper sense of fulfillment and motivation.

- Customers can sense when a business genuinely cares about providing value versus when it's solely motivated by profit. Authenticity breeds trust and loyalty.

- Instead of chasing short-term profits, focus on building long-lasting customer relationships and connections. Sustainable success comes from creating real, tangible value.

- Understand that wealth is a byproduct of creating value. Prioritize value creation, knowing that wealth will naturally follow because of your efforts.

- Success in entrepreneurship should be measured by financial gains and the positive impact you make on the world and the fulfillment you derive from your work.

Conclusion

As I stood in the parking lot, surveying the results of a day's hard work, I couldn't help but reflect on the journey that led me here. Being the owner of a thriving car detailing business isn't just about turning a profit; it's about embracing the process, the challenges, and the victories that come with entrepreneurship.

I remember the early days when I would spend countless hours perfecting my craft, fueled by a passion for cars and a drive to create something of my own. There were setbacks, as you know—times when I questioned whether I had what it took to succeed, especially after failing in the food and beverage space. But with each challenge, I learned invaluable lessons about resilience, determination, and the importance of staying true to my values as a business owner.

One memory stands out—a hot summer's day when a loyal customer brought in his beloved classic car for full detailing. As we meticulously polished every inch of that vintage beauty, I saw the joy in his eyes and felt a sense of pride, knowing that we had exceeded his expectations. Moments like these reminded me of why I had embarked on this journey in the first place—to serve clients by doing what I love and aspiring to provide exceptional value to the world in ways they couldn't find anywhere else.

But the way I reached that end goal wasn't just by starting a business and seeing success right away. It was by embracing the process. It's in the process where you will spend 99% of your time, so you must embrace it. It is the process that must provide you with joy, and fulfillment as opposed to the big milestones.

If you can find joy in the process of being an entrepreneur and building a business, it will increase your productivity and the quality of the work you produce. Following the process and consistently doing the correct actions will naturally lead to the outcomes you seek as an entrepreneur. The joy in the process is what will make you persevere and persist with this journey and will give you the longevity that will bring long-term success. Think of the goal of losing weight. Following a process that you dislike will surely lead to failure in the long run, as you're unlikely to stick with it for an extended period. However, if you find something that you enjoy, say playing a sport or doing a dance class, you have now found joy in the process and will focus on the activity rather than the outcome. Losing weight will be the natural result of the process but will not be your sole focus.

Embracing the process is the only way to continually grow as an entrepreneur. By seeing setbacks as opportunities for growth, I refined my own business to be the best in the market. I enjoyed the process of not only improving the skills

I already had but also learning entirely new skills for building and running a new business.

Savor the experiences and never lose sight of what motivated you to start in the first place. I hope you find as much fulfillment in your new business as I have mine, and more importantly, the process of creating it, improving your skills, and experimenting over time. Each day I get to work on my business, I thank myself for choosing this life and I know deep down that it was meant for me. I sense you feel the same.

The purpose of this book was to provide you with the tools to become a successful entrepreneur and give you a step-by-step guide to start a business today. Now, armed with the insights and strategies shared throughout this book, you have all the tools you need to embark on your journey as a successful entrepreneur. Whether your passion lies in dropshipping, digital products, an online agency, or any other area, the principles of entrepreneurship remain the same. Remember, this is just the start of your business journey. While the ideas and tools we have discussed are your launchpad to greater things, you still need to continue to learn and develop deeper skills to realize your ambitions. With a commitment to providing value, you have the power and control to change your world. It's up to you now to take action to bring your dreams to life.

Remember, to start and win in business, you must make it a matter of life or death. You cannot be half-hearted. Recognize the necessity of wholehearted commitment to entrepreneurship. It is the realization of this commitment that is the only way to change your circumstances and bring all the positive benefits that wealth has to offer.

Cultivating an entrepreneurial mindset involves embracing failure as an opportunity for growth, thinking creatively, and continuously seeking ways to innovate and improve. By adopting this mindset, you enhance your chances of success in business and life, empowering yourself to overcome obstacles and achieve your goals with confidence and determination. Throughout my years of running a business, I've found that these skills are not only helpful at work but in all facets of my life.

On top of developing an entrepreneurial mindset, it's important to have a single focus to achieve success. Mastery comes from mastering one area of expertise. Just like I built my business based on my existing skills in car detailing, build your business on a particular skill or interest you already have. Make your focus narrow and it will be much easier to carve out a niche for yourself.

Keep in mind that instead of focusing solely on creating a product or service, shift your attention to developing a robust and scalable system that can run and grow your business efficiently. Remember that a business system encompasses everything from your processes and workflows to your team structure and customer interactions. By building a solid foundation and implementing systems that streamline operations, you create a framework that allows your business to thrive and expand without solely relying on your direct involvement.

Think of your business system as the engine that powers your enterprise, allowing you to delegate tasks, scale your operations, and adapt to changing market conditions with ease. By investing time and resources into designing and optimizing your systems, you increase your business's value and free up your time to focus on strategic growth initiatives and personal fulfillment. This also ensures that your business can withstand the tests of time and continue to thrive well into the future.

As you move into the process of starting your business, keep in mind our VANS criteria. It must be Viable, Autonomous, fulfill a Need, and be Scalable. When you focus on your area of interest, ensure that it meets the VANS criteria, and test it incrementally to ensure that it's viable. Your chances of success are already much higher than the average aspiring entrepreneur.

Embracing failure and building skills will always be necessary. Testing the viability of your business in increments is the best way to go, and continuous refinements and adjustments will likely be needed. This is why it's helpful to focus on one area of expertise. It will be much easier to become a master at your business. This way, when setbacks come up, you can improve your expertise in that one area and continue to be the go-to business for your ideal customers, providing value that they can't find anywhere else.

You must place value creation at the center of everything you do. And the value you create must be exceptional. The magnitude of value and the breadth of people it affects will determine the level of success you achieve. Don't offer an average value proposition, and make sure it is remarkable.

Now is the time to turn inspiration into action. Take that favorite business idea you've been nurturing and start putting it to the test. As mentioned in my previous book, you also hold the power to shape your financial future. By taking control of your destiny and pursuing entrepreneurship, you create opportunities for growth, prosperity, and freedom over your entire lifestyle. Embrace the journey with confidence, knowing that every mistake is a learning opportunity that can bring you closer to your goals and build your charisma as a human being.

If you'd like to take another step toward total financial freedom, join me in my previous book, *9 Money Habits Keeping You Poor*, where we review the nine financial habits preventing you from being financially free and how to move past them. This book has been especially helpful for those embarking on entrepreneurial ventures.

Before we part ways for now, I want to express my deepest gratitude for your engagement, dedication, and willingness to build a business. Your commitment to self-improvement and entrepreneurship is truly inspiring, and the world needs entrepreneurs like you to continually push the boundaries of what's possible. Remember, no matter where your journey takes you, you're never alone. Here's to your success, fulfillment, and prosperity. Thank you for joining me in this incredible adventure.

References

Barral, J. (2018). "Neuroentrepreneurship: What Can Entrepreneurship Learn from Neuroscience?" Frontiers in Psychology, 9, 1436. DOI: 10.3389/fpsyg.2018.01436

DeBevoise, N. (2023). "Decisions Are for Suckers: Avoid Decision Fatigue." Forbes. https://www.forbes.com/sites/nelldebevoise/2023/10/27/decisions-are-for-suckers-avoid-decision-fatigue/?sh=4f90c2554364

Dividend Real Estate. "7 Income Streams of Millionaires: An Open Discussion." https://dividendrealestate.com/7incomestreams/

Finkelstein, S., Hambrick, D. C., & Cannella Jr, A. A. (2009). "Strategic Leadership: Theory and Research on Executives, Top Management Teams, and Boards." Oxford University Press.

Gale, W. (2019). "Chipping Away at the Mortgage Deduction." Brookings. https://www.brookings.edu/opinions/chipping-away-at-the-mortgage-deduction/

Gallup. (2015). "Delegating: A Huge Management Challenge for Entrepreneurs." https://news.gallup.com/businessjournal/182414/delegating-huge-management-challenge-entrepreneurs.aspx

Gannon, B. (2022). "How Decision Fatigue Can Make or Break a Startup." https://www.forbes.com/sites/forbesbusinesscouncil/2022/02/15/how-decision-fatigue-can-make-or-break-a-startup/?sh=3fd70283155e

Glaub, M., Frese, M., Fischer, S., & Hoppe, M. (2014). "Increasing Personal Initiative in Small Business Managers or Owners Leads to Entrepreneurial Success: A Theory-Based Controlled Randomized Field Intervention for Evidence-Based Management." Academy of Management Learning & Education, 13(3), 354-379. DOI: 10.5465/amle.2013.0025

Global Entrepreneurship Monitor. (2023). "Latest Global Entrepreneurship Report." https://www.gemconsortium.org/reports/latest-global-report

Harvard Business Review. (2016). "The Impact of Employee Engagement on Performance." https://hbr.org/sponsored/2016/04/the-impact-of-employee-engagement-on-performance

Kenton, W. (2023). "The Rule of 72: Definition, Usefulness, and How to Use It." Investopedia. https://www.investopedia.com/terms/r/ruleof72.asp

Markides, C. (1997). "To Diversify or Not to Diversify." Harvard Business Review. https://hbr.org/1997/11/to-diversify-or-not-to-diversify

Moon, G. (2021). "Nike Marketing Strategy: How to Build a Timeless Brand." CoSchedule Blog. https://coschedule.com/blog/nike-marketing-strategy

PR Newswire. (2024). "Corporate E-learning Market Size to Record USD 153.41 Billion Growth from 2024-2028." https://www.prnewswire.com/news-releases/corporate-e-learning-market-size-to-record-usd-153-41-billion-growth-from-2024-2028--technavio-302138364.html

Printful. "Is Print on Demand Worth It?" https://www.print-ful.com/blog/is-print-on-demand-worth-it

Salesforce. (2021). "State of the Connected Customer Report Outlines Changing Standards for Customer Engagement." https://www.salesforce.com/news/stories/state-of-the-con-nected-customer-report-outlines-changing-standards-for-cus-tomer-engagement/

Segal, T. (2024). "Profit Margin: Definition, Types, Uses in Busi-ness and Investing. https://www.in-vestopedia.com/terms/p/profitmargin.asp

Sirohi, A. (2023). "What Is the Average Email Marketing ROI?" Constant Contact. https://www.constantcon-tact.com/blog/what-is-the-roi-of-email-marketing/S

Statista. "Online Advertising Spending Worldwide." https://www.statista.com/statistics/237974/online-advertising-spending-worldwide/

StaxBill. "Subscription Businesses and Global Emissions Tar-gets." https://staxbill.com/subscription-businesses-global-emis-sions-targets/

Yin, R. K. (2018). "Case Study Research and Applications: Design and Methods." SAGE Publications.

Zhou, L. "Small Business Statistics." https://www.luisa-zhou.com/blog/small-business-statistics/

About the Author

Adam Rose, the mastermind behind *9 Money Habits Keeping You Poor: My Story to Financial Freedom*, is poised to make a lasting impact on readers. Through his writing, Adam aims to inspire and empower readers, enabling them to embark on their own path to financial freedom.

Adam holds a bachelor's degree in economics, specializing in financial planning and investment strategies. Additionally, Adam holds a master's degree in business administration with a concentration in finance.

Adam likes to draw from his life experiences to enrich each narrative and share the lessons that he's learned firsthand. For instance, after working in a car dealership, he recognized an opportunity and started his own successful car detailing company. This entrepreneurial endeavor allowed him to gain practical knowledge about running a business, managing finances, and achieving profitability. Through his professional endeavors, Adam has had the opportunity to collaborate with individuals from diverse financial backgrounds, enabling him to develop a comprehensive understanding of the challenges people face on their financial journey.

Married to Thea and a devoted parent to three children, Adam is determined to help others take control of their lives by sharing his personal journey and reflecting on his transformations.

.